According to Jesus...

His Messages for the 21st Century

Steven Smith

Sherwood Press

Contents

Love and Compassion in a Diverse World

Inclusivity, Tolerance and Supporting the Marginalized

Inclusivity and Tolerance

Inclusivity and tolerance are fundamental aspects of Jesus' teachings and are critical for fostering a harmonious and respectful society. Let's delve deeper into these principles and explore their implications for our modern world.

1. Understanding Jesus' Command to Love

Jesus' commandment, "Love your neighbor as yourself" (Matthew 22:39), is central to His message. This directive goes beyond mere tolerance and calls for active, empathetic love towards others. It means treating others with the same kindness, respect, and consideration we desire for ourselves.

- **Empathy and Understanding**: Loving others as ourselves requires us to put ourselves in their shoes. It involves understanding their struggles, joys, and perspectives. This approach helps us connect with people on a deeper level, fostering genuine relationships and reducing conflicts.

2. Breaking Down Prejudices

Jesus often challenged societal norms and prejudices. He interacted with marginalized people, such as tax collectors, Samaritans, and women, showing that God's love is inclusive and boundless.

- **Example of the Samaritan Woman**: In John 4, Jesus speaks with a Samaritan woman at the well, breaking several cultural taboos. Jews typically avoided Samaritans, and men did not speak publicly with women. By engaging with her, Jesus demonstrated that His message and love are for everyone, regardless of social barriers.

- **Challenging Racism and Xenophobia**: Modern applications of this principle include combating racism and xenophobia. Recognizing the inherent worth of every person, regardless of their race or nationality, is a step towards building a more inclusive society.

3. Promoting Equality

Jesus' teachings advocate for the equal treatment of all people. He emphasized that in God's kingdom, traditional social hierarchies are overturned.

- **The Beatitudes**: In the Beatitudes (Matthew 5:3-12), Jesus blesses the poor in spirit, the meek, and those who hunger for righteousness. This message upends the values of a society that often honors the wealthy and powerful. By valuing those who are typically overlooked, Jesus promotes a radical equality.

- **Modern Social Equality**: Today, this principle can inspire efforts to achieve gender equality, LGBTQ+ rights, and the fair treatment of people with disabilities. By ensuring that everyone has the same opportunities and rights, we honor the inclusive nature of Jesus' teachings.

4. Building Inclusive Communities

Inclusivity means creating spaces where everyone feels welcome and valued. Jesus' approach to community was inclusive, breaking down barriers and inviting everyone to join.

- **Table Fellowship**: Jesus often dined with sinners and outcasts (Luke 5:29-32). These meals were symbolic of the inclusive nature of God's kingdom, where everyone is invited to the table.

- **Community Building**: In modern terms, this can be seen in efforts to create inclusive schools, workplaces, and neighborhoods. Policies that ensure diversity and prevent discrimination are vital for fostering inclusive communities.

5. Tolerance and Respect for Differences

Tolerance involves respecting and valuing differences rather than merely enduring them. It requires an open-minded approach and a willingness to learn from others.

- **The Golden Rule**: Jesus' teaching of the Golden Rule, "Do to others as you would have them do to you" (Luke 6:31), encapsulates this idea. It calls for mutual respect and fair treatment, which are essential for peaceful coexistence.

- **Interfaith Dialogue**: In today's diverse world, tolerance is particularly important in interfaith contexts. Engaging in respectful dialogue with people of different religious beliefs promotes mutual understanding and reduces conflict.

6. Active Engagement and Advocacy

Inclusivity and tolerance also mean actively working to dismantle systems of oppression and advocating for those who are marginalized.

- **Jesus as an Advocate**: Jesus stood up for the marginalized, like when He defended the woman caught in adultery (John 8:1-11). He challenged those in power and advocated for the oppressed.

- **Modern Advocacy**: This can inspire modern efforts to fight against systemic injustices such as poverty, racism, and inequality. Advocacy involves raising awareness and pushing for policy changes promoting social justice.

7. Fostering a Culture of Inclusion

Creating an inclusive culture means inclusivity becomes a fundamental value in all aspects of life. This culture promotes a sense of belonging for everyone.

- **Church as a Model**: The early Christian church modeled inclusivity, bringing together Jews and Gentiles, rich and poor, men and women (Galatians 3:28). This diverse community reflected the inclusive nature of God's kingdom.

- **Inclusive Practices**: In contemporary settings, this might involve implementing inclusive practices in education, healthcare, and government. Training programs on diversity and inclusion can help foster environments where everyone feels valued and respected.

8. The Role of Forgiveness in Inclusivity

Forgiveness plays a crucial role in promoting inclusivity and tolerance. By forgiving others, we can overcome past grievances and build more inclusive relationships.

- **Jesus on Forgiveness**: Jesus taught that we should forgive others, not just once, but seventy-seven times (Matthew 18:22). This radical forgiveness helps heal divisions and fosters a more inclusive community.

- **Reconciliation Efforts**: Forgiveness is vital in reconciliation efforts, whether in personal relationships or broader societal contexts. Truth and reconciliation commissions, like those in South Africa, show how forgiveness can help heal historical injustices and promote inclusive societies.

<u>Supporting the Marginalized</u>

Supporting the marginalized is a central theme in Jesus' teachings. His actions and parables often highlighted the importance of caring for those who are overlooked, oppressed, or in need. Let's explore this concept in greater detail, considering its implications for both personal behavior and societal structures.

1. The Parable of the Good Samaritan

The Parable of the Good Samaritan (Luke 10:25-37) is one of Jesus' most powerful teachings on supporting the marginalized. This parable tells the story of a man who is beaten and left for dead on the side of the road. A priest and a Levite pass by without helping, but a Samaritan stops to assist the injured man, providing medical care and ensuring his safety.

- **Challenging Social Norms**: Samaritans were despised by Jews in Jesus' time, making the Samaritan an unlikely hero. By using a Samaritan as the example of compassion, Jesus challenges his listeners to reconsider their prejudices and extend love to all, regardless of societal boundaries.

- **Active Compassion**: The Samaritan's actions illustrate that true compassion involves more than just feeling pity. It requires taking concrete steps to help those in need, even if it involves personal sacrifice.

2. Jesus' Ministry to the Marginalized

Throughout His ministry, Jesus actively sought out and ministered to those who were marginalized by society.

- **Healing the Sick**: Jesus often healed those who were sick and considered outcasts. For example, He healed lepers (Luke 17:11-19) and the blind (John 9:1-7), restoring their health and their place in the community.

- **Eating with Sinners**: Jesus frequently dined with tax collectors and sinners (Matthew 9:10-13). By doing so, He showed that God's love extends to everyone, including those who were socially ostracized.

- **Defending the Oppressed**: In the story of the woman caught in adultery (John 8:1-11), Jesus defended her against those who sought to condemn her, demonstrating mercy and compassion instead of judgment.

3. Promoting Social Justice

Jesus' teachings encourage us to advocate for social justice and work towards a society where everyone is treated fairly.

- **The Beatitudes**: In the Beatitudes (Matthew 5:3-12), Jesus blesses the poor, the meek, and those who hunger for righteousness. This teaching highlights God's concern for the oppressed and marginalized.

- **Advocacy for the Poor**: Jesus' concern for the poor is evident in His teachings, such as when He said, "Blessed are you who are poor, for yours is the kingdom of God" (Luke 6:20). This emphasis on the poor challenges us to advocate for economic justice and support policies that address poverty and inequality.

4. Providing Practical Assistance

Supporting the marginalized involves providing practical assistance to meet their immediate needs.

- **Feeding the Hungry**: Jesus fed the hungry on several occasions, such as the feeding of the 5,000 (Matthew 14:13-21). This act of compassion emphasizes the importance of meeting the basic needs of those who are hungry.

- **Clothing the Naked**: In the parable of the sheep and the goats (Matthew 25:31-46), Jesus describes how caring for the needy is akin to caring for Him. Providing clothing, shelter, and other necessities to those in need is a direct way to live out His teachings.

5. Empowering the Marginalized

In addition to providing immediate assistance, supporting the marginalized also involves empowering them to improve their circumstances.

- **Education and Skill Development**: Empowering marginalized individuals through education and skill development can help them achieve long-term self-sufficiency. This might involve supporting programs that provide job training, literacy education, and other resources.

- **Advocacy and Legal Support**: Marginalized groups often face systemic barriers. Providing legal support and advocating for their rights can help dismantle these barriers and promote greater equality.

6. Creating Inclusive Communities

Jesus' teachings call for the creation of inclusive communities where everyone is valued and accepted.

- **Welcoming the Stranger**: In Matthew 25:35, Jesus says, "I was a stranger and you welcomed me." This teaching encourages us to be hospitable and inclusive, creating communities where everyone feels welcome.

- **Building Inclusive Institutions**: Schools, workplaces, and other institutions should strive to be inclusive, ensuring that marginalized individuals have equal opportunities to participate and thrive.

7. Addressing Systemic Injustices

Supporting the marginalized also involves addressing the systemic injustices that contribute to their marginalization.

- **Racial Injustice**: Jesus' teachings on love and equality challenge us to confront and dismantle systemic racism. This involves advocating for policies promoting racial equality and eliminating discriminatory practices.

- **Economic Inequality**: Addressing economic inequality requires advocating for fair wages, access to healthcare, affordable housing, and other measures that support economic justice.

8. Engaging in Compassionate Advocacy

Compassionate advocacy involves standing up for those who cannot advocate for themselves and working to create a more just society.

- **Voice for the Voiceless**: Proverbs 31:8-9 says, "Speak up for those who cannot speak for themselves, for the rights of all who are destitute. Speak up and judge fairly; defend the rights of the poor and needy." This aligns with Jesus' call to support the marginalized.

- **Long-term Commitment**: Advocacy requires a long-term commitment to justice and equality. This might involve participating in advocacy groups, writing to policymakers, and raising awareness about social issues.

9. Reflecting God's Love and Justice

Ultimately, supporting the marginalized reflects God's love and justice in the world.

- **Living Out the Gospel**: By caring for the marginalized, we live out the gospel message and reflect God's character. Micah 6:8 says, "He has shown you, O mortal, what is good. And what does the Lord require of you? To act justly and to love mercy and to walk humbly with your God."

- **Being Christ-like**: Jesus' entire ministry was characterized by compassion and justice. Following His example means prioritizing the needs of the marginalized and working to create a more just and loving world.

Conclusion

Inclusivity and Tolerance

In summary, the teachings of Jesus on inclusivity and tolerance provide a vital blueprint for building a harmonious and respectful society. His command to "love your neighbor as yourself" (Matthew 22:39) calls for an empathetic, active love that transcends social, racial, and cultural boundaries. By breaking down prejudices, promoting equality, and fostering inclusive communities, we can create environments where everyone feels valued and accepted. Respecting differences, engaging in interfaith dialogue, and advocating for the marginalized are all essential steps in living out Jesus' message. Embracing these principles helps build a world that reflects the inclusivity and compassion of God's kingdom, where mutual respect and understanding pave the way for true social harmony.

Supporting the Marginalized

Supporting the marginalized is a core tenet of Jesus' teachings, exemplified through His parables, actions, and direct instructions. The Parable of the Good Samaritan (Luke 10:25-37) and Jesus' ministry to the outcasts illustrate the importance of active compassion and breaking down societal barriers. By promoting social justice, providing practical assistance, empowering the marginalized, and addressing systemic injustices, we honor Jesus' call to care for the least among us. Engaging in compassionate advocacy and building inclusive communities reflect God's love and justice, encouraging a more equitable and loving world. As followers of Jesus, it is our duty to support those in need and work towards a society where everyone is treated with dignity and respect, embodying the principles of the gospel in our daily lives.

Reflection Questions

Reflecting on the principles of inclusivity, tolerance, and supporting the marginalized can help deepen understanding and encourage the practical application of these concepts. Here are some questions for reflection:

Inclusivity and Tolerance

1. **Personal Biases**: Are there any personal biases or prejudices that you need to confront and overcome? How can you actively work towards being more inclusive in your interactions with others?

2. **Understanding Others**: How well do you understand the cultural, religious, or personal backgrounds of those around you? What steps can you take to learn more about and appreciate these differences?

3. **Acts of Inclusion**: What are some concrete actions you can take to promote inclusivity and tolerance in your community, school, or workplace?

4. **Overcoming Stereotypes**: How can you challenge and change stereotypes or assumptions you

might hold about others? What practices can help you see people as individuals rather than categories?

5. **Role Models**: Who are the role models of inclusivity and tolerance in your life or community? What can you learn from their example?

Supporting the Marginalized

1. **Awareness of Marginalization**: Who are your community's marginalized individuals or groups? How can you become more aware of their needs and challenges?

2. **Empathy and Action**: How can you cultivate empathy for marginalized people? What specific actions can you take to support and uplift them?

3. **Community Involvement**: How can you get involved in community efforts to support the marginalized? Are there organizations or initiatives you can join or support?

4. **Advocacy**: How can you use your voice and resources to advocate for social justice and the rights of marginalized individuals? What issues are you passionate about, and how can you contribute to positive change?

5. **Personal Responsibility**: How can you take personal responsibility for addressing injustice

and supporting the marginalized in your everyday life? How can you consistently embody compassion and support?

Reflecting on these questions can help individuals understand and apply the principles of love, compassion, inclusivity, and support for the marginalized in their daily lives. By doing so, they can create a more just, empathetic, and cohesive society.

Forgiveness and Reconciliation

Healing Divisions and Restorative Justice

Healing Divisions

Forgiveness and reconciliation are at the heart of Jesus' teachings and are crucial for healing divisions in our world. In a society often torn apart by conflict, grudges, and misunderstandings, Jesus' emphasis on forgiveness offers a pathway to restore relationships and build a more peaceful community. Let's delve into the concept of healing divisions in greater detail.

1. The Importance of Forgiveness

Jesus placed a strong emphasis on the necessity of forgiveness for healing divisions. In Matthew 6:14-15, He says, "For if you forgive others their trespasses, your heavenly Father will also forgive you; but if you do not forgive others their trespasses, neither will your Father forgive your trespasses."

- **Personal Healing**: Forgiveness is essential for personal healing. Holding onto grudges and resentment can be emotionally and physically damaging. By forgiving others, we release the burden of anger and make space for peace and healing in our own lives.

- **Restoring Relationships**: Forgiveness is the first step toward reconciliation. It opens the door for dialogue and understanding, helping to restore broken relationships and heal emotional wounds.

2. Jesus' Teachings on Forgiveness

Jesus' teachings provide clear guidance on the practice of forgiveness and its role in healing divisions.

- **Seventy-Seven Times**: In Matthew 18:21-22, Peter asks Jesus how many times he should forgive someone who sins against him. Jesus replies, "I tell you, not seven times, but seventy-seven times." This signifies that forgiveness should be boundless and ongoing.

- **The Parable of the Unforgiving Servant**: In Matthew 18:23-35, Jesus tells a parable about a servant who, despite being forgiven a massive debt by his master, refuses to forgive a small debt owed to him by a fellow servant. This parable illustrates the importance of extending the same mercy and forgiveness we receive to others.

3. Practical Steps to Forgiveness

Healing divisions through forgiveness involves practical steps that can be implemented in everyday life.

- **Acknowledgment**: The first step in forgiveness is acknowledging the hurt or offense. It is essential to recognize and validate the pain before moving towards forgiveness.

- **Empathy and Understanding**: Try to understand the perspective of the person who caused the hurt. Empathy can foster compassion and make it easier to forgive.

- **Communication**: Open and honest communication is crucial for reconciliation. Discussing the issue with the other person can clear up misunderstandings and pave the way for healing.

- **Letting Go of Resentment**: Forgiveness involves letting go of grudges and resentment. This doesn't mean forgetting the offense but rather releasing its negative emotions.

- **Seeking Forgiveness**: Just as important as forgiving others is seeking forgiveness when we have wronged someone. This act of humility can repair relationships and heal divisions.

4. Reconciliation in Communities

Healing divisions extend beyond personal relationships to communities and larger social groups.

- **Community Dialogue**: Facilitating dialogue within communities can help address collective grievances and misunderstandings. Community forums, peace talks, and reconciliation commissions can be effective in promoting healing.

- **Restorative Justice**: Restorative justice practices focus on repairing the harm caused by criminal behavior through reconciliation between the victim and the offender. This approach emphasizes healing rather than punishment and has been successful in various contexts worldwide.

- **Cultural Understanding**: Promoting cultural understanding and appreciation can help heal divisions in diverse communities. Educational programs, cultural exchanges, and interfaith dialogues are valuable tools in this regard.

5. International Reconciliation

On a global scale, forgiveness and reconciliation are essential for healing divisions between nations and cultures.

- **Historical Injustices**: Addressing historical injustices and acknowledging past wrongs is crucial for reconciliation between nations. Apologies, reparations, and truth-telling processes are steps towards healing.

- **Peacebuilding Initiatives**: International organizations and peacebuilding initiatives work towards reconciliation in conflict zones. These efforts often include dialogue, negotiation, and collaborative problem-solving to foster long-term peace.

- **Promoting Diplomacy**: Diplomatic efforts that prioritize understanding, respect, and forgiveness can prevent conflicts and promote harmonious international relations.

6. The Role of the Church

The Church plays a significant role in promoting forgiveness and reconciliation.

- **Teaching and Preaching**: Churches can teach about the importance of forgiveness through sermons, Bible studies, and educational programs, emphasizing Jesus' teachings on the subject.

- **Counseling and Support**: Offering counseling and support services for individuals struggling with forgiveness can help them on their journey toward healing.

- **Community Outreach**: Churches can engage in outreach programs promoting reconciliation and healing within local contexts.

7. Personal Testimonies of Forgiveness

Stories and testimonies of forgiveness can inspire others to pursue healing and reconciliation.

- **Examples of Forgiveness**: Sharing stories of individuals who have experienced profound forgiveness can provide hope and motivation for others. These testimonies demonstrate the transformative power of forgiveness.

- **Encouraging Forgiveness**: Encouraging people to share their own journeys of forgiveness can create a supportive community and promote a culture of reconciliation.

8. Biblical Examples of Forgiveness

The Bible provides numerous examples of forgiveness that can guide us in healing divisions.

- **Joseph and His Brothers**: In Genesis 50:15-21, Joseph forgives his brothers who sold him into slavery. His forgiveness and reconciliation with his family highlight the power of letting go of past wrongs and restoring relationships.

- **Jesus on the Cross**: One of the most profound examples of forgiveness is Jesus on the cross, asking God to forgive those who crucified Him, saying, "Father, forgive them, for they do not know what they are doing" (Luke 23:34). This ultimate act of forgiveness sets a powerful example for us to follow.

9. Forgiveness and Mental Health

Forgiveness also has significant benefits for mental health and well-being.

- **Reducing Stress**: Letting go of grudges and resentment can reduce stress and anxiety, leading to better overall mental health.

- **Promoting Inner Peace**: Forgiveness fosters a sense of inner peace and emotional stability, contributing to a healthier and more balanced life.

- **Improving Relationships**: Forgiveness can improve interpersonal relationships, leading to a more supportive and positive social environment.

Restorative Justice

Restorative justice is a concept that aligns closely with Jesus' teachings, focusing on healing and reconciliation rather than punishment and retribution. It seeks to repair the harm caused by wrongdoing through inclusive processes that engage victims, offenders, and the community. Jesus' teachings, especially the story of the Prodigal Son, highlight the transformative power of mercy and the importance of restorative practices. Let's explore the concept of restorative justice in greater detail.

1. Understanding Restorative Justice

Restorative justice is a process that brings together those affected by wrongdoing to address the harm, seek accountability, and promote healing.

- **Victim-Centered Approach**: This approach prioritizes the needs and experiences of victims, ensuring they have a voice in the justice process. It seeks to provide victims with a sense of closure and empowerment.

- **Offender Accountability**: Restorative justice requires offenders to take responsibility for their actions and understand the impact of their behavior on others. This accountability is crucial for genuine repentance and transformation.

- **Community Involvement**: The community plays a significant role in restorative justice, helping to support both the victim and the offender and working to prevent future harm.

2. Biblical Foundations

Jesus' teachings provide a strong foundation for restorative justice, emphasizing forgiveness, mercy, and reconciliation.

- **The Prodigal Son**: In Luke 15:11-32, Jesus tells the story of a father who forgives his wayward son and welcomes him back with open arms. This parable highlights the themes of repentance, forgiveness, and reconciliation. The father's willingness to forgive and restore his son to the family reflects the essence of restorative justice.

- **Forgiveness of Sins**: Jesus often forgave sins and encouraged others to do the same. In John 8:1-11, He forgives a woman caught in adultery, demonstrating mercy and offering her a chance for a new beginning.

3. Principles of Restorative Justice

Restorative justice operates on several key principles that align with Jesus' teachings.

- **Repairing Harm**: The primary goal is to repair the harm caused by wrongdoing. This involves addressing the needs of the victim, helping the offender understand the impact of their actions, and restoring relationships.

- **Inclusive Decision-Making**: Restorative justice involves all stakeholders in the process, including victims, offenders, and community members. This inclusive approach ensures that everyone's voice is heard and respected.

- **Transformation and Healing**: The focus is on healing and transformation rather than punishment. This principle aligns with Jesus' message of redemption and new beginnings.

4. Practical Applications

Restorative justice can be applied in various contexts, including criminal justice, schools, and communities.

- **Criminal Justice**: In the criminal justice system, restorative justice can take the form of victim-offender mediation, restorative circles, and community conferencing. These practices provide a space for victims to express their feelings, for offenders to take responsibility, and for the community to support the healing process.

- **Schools**: Restorative practices in schools can help address conflicts and behavioral issues. Techniques such as restorative circles and peer mediation promote a positive school climate, reduce bullying, and improve student relationships.

- **Community Programs**: Community-based restorative justice programs address local conflicts and issues. These programs often involve mediation and community service, helping rebuild community trust and cohesion.

5. Benefits of Restorative Justice

Restorative justice offers numerous benefits for victims, offenders, and communities.

- **Empowerment for Victims**: Victims are given a voice and an active role in the justice process, helping them regain a sense of control and closure.

- **Offender Rehabilitation**: Offenders are encouraged to understand the impact of their actions, take responsibility, and make amends. This process can lead to genuine remorse and reduce recidivism.

- **Community Strengthening**: By involving the community in the justice process, restorative justice helps build stronger, more cohesive communities. It fosters mutual respect, understanding, and cooperation.

6. Challenges and Considerations

Implementing restorative justice is not without challenges. It requires careful planning and a commitment to the principles of inclusivity and fairness.

- **Ensuring Participation**: It is crucial to ensure that all parties, especially victims, participate voluntarily and feel safe throughout the process. Coercion can undermine the effectiveness of restorative justice.

- **Balancing Needs**: The needs of victims and offenders must be balanced carefully. While addressing the harm and holding offenders accountable is important, the process must also be fair and supportive for all involved.

- **Building Trust**: Restorative justice relies on trust and openness. Building trust between victims, offenders, and the community can be challenging, especially in cases involving severe harm or deep-seated conflicts.

7. Restorative Justice in Practice

Examples of successful restorative justice practices demonstrate their potential to transform lives and communities.

- **Victim-Offender Mediation Programs**: Programs like the Victim-Offender Reconciliation Program (VORP) provide structured settings for victims and offenders to discuss the impact of the crime and agree on restitution. These programs have shown positive outcomes in terms of victim satisfaction and offender accountability.

- **Community Conferencing**: In some communities, restorative justice takes the form of community conferencing, where all stakeholders come together to discuss the harm and develop a plan for restitution. This approach fosters community involvement and shared responsibility for resolving conflicts.

- **Restorative Schools**: Schools that have adopted restorative practices report reductions in disciplinary issues and improvements in school climate. Techniques like restorative circles allow students to address conflicts and build stronger, more supportive relationships.

8. Theological Reflections on Restorative Justice

From a theological perspective, restorative justice reflects God's nature and the gospel's transformative power.

- **God's Mercy and Justice**: Restorative justice embodies the balance of God's mercy and justice. It seeks to restore relationships and promote healing, reflecting the divine desire for reconciliation.

- **The Ministry of Reconciliation**: In 2 Corinthians 5:18-19, Paul speaks of the ministry of reconciliation, stating that God reconciled us to Himself through Christ and gave us the ministry of reconciliation. Restorative justice is a practical expression of this ministry, promoting healing and wholeness in relationships and communities.

Conclusion

Healing Divisions

Healing divisions through forgiveness and reconciliation is vital to Jesus' teachings. By embracing forgiveness, acknowledging past hurts, and taking practical steps toward reconciliation, we can restore personal relationships and promote peace within communities and nations. Jesus' examples, such as forgiving those who wronged Him and the parable of the Prodigal Son, provide powerful inspiration for practicing forgiveness in our own lives. As we work towards healing divisions, we foster harmony and understanding, reflecting the love and mercy that Jesus exemplified. Embracing these principles, we build a more compassionate and united world grounded in justice, empathy, and reconciliation.

Restorative Justice

Restorative justice, deeply rooted in the teachings of Jesus, offers a transformative approach to addressing harm and promoting healing. It prioritizes repairing relationships, holding offenders accountable, and involving the community, aligning with the principles of mercy, forgiveness, and reconciliation central to the gospel. Restorative justice promotes a more compassionate and equitable world by empowering victims, rehabilitating offenders, and strengthening social bonds. This approach reflects God's love and justice, encouraging us to heal divisions and build a society where forgiveness and reconciliation are at the heart of justice. We can work towards a more inclusive, understanding, and supportive community through restorative justice.

Reflection Questions

Reflecting on the principles of forgiveness and reconciliation, particularly in healing divisions and restorative justice contexts, can help deepen understanding and encourage the practical application of these concepts. Here are some questions for reflection:

Healing Divisions

1. **Personal Grudges**: Do you need to address any grudges or unresolved conflicts in your life? How can you take steps towards forgiveness and reconciliation in these situations?

2. **Empathy and Understanding**: How can you better understand the perspectives and experiences of those you have conflicts with? What actions can you take to foster empathy and mutual understanding?

3. **Communication**: How effective is your communication when dealing with conflicts? What strategies can you implement to improve open, honest, and compassionate dialogue?

4. **Reconciliation Efforts**: Have you ever witnessed or been part of a successful reconciliation effort? What lessons did you learn from that experience, and how can you apply them to other situations?

5. **Role Models**: Who are the role models of forgiveness and reconciliation in your life or community? What can you learn from their example?

Restorative Justice

1. **Understanding Impact**: How well do you understand the impact of your actions on others, both positive and negative? How can you improve your awareness and sensitivity to this impact?

2. **Taking Responsibility**: Are there situations where you need to take responsibility for your actions and seek to make amends? What steps can you take to address these situations?

3. **Supporting Others**: How can you support others in your community who have been harmed by wrongdoing? What role can you play in helping to facilitate healing and reconciliation?

4. **Community Involvement**: How can you get involved in restorative justice initiatives in your community? Are there programs or organizations you can join or support?

5. **Personal Growth**: How has reflecting on forgiveness and accountability helped you grow as a person? What ongoing practices can you implement to ensure you continue to prioritize these values in your life?

Reflecting on these questions can help individuals understand and apply the principles of forgiveness and reconciliation in their daily lives. By doing so, they can create a more compassionate, just, and harmonious society.

Ethical Leadership and Integrity

Servant Leadership and Integrity and Accountability

Servant Leadership

Servant leadership is a leadership philosophy that emphasizes the leader's role as a servant first. This concept aligns closely with Jesus' teachings and actions, as He consistently modeled servant leadership throughout His ministry. By focusing on serving others, rather than exerting power over them, servant leaders can foster trust, collaboration, and a sense of community. Let's explore the subtopic of servant leadership in greater detail.

1. Jesus' Teaching on Servant Leadership

Jesus directly taught about servant leadership, particularly in response to His disciples' arguments about who among them was the greatest.
  - **Matthew 20:26-28**: "Whoever wants to become great among you must be your servant, and whoever wants to be first must be your slave—just as the Son of Man did not come to be served, but to serve, and to give His life as a ransom for many."

- **Greatness Through Service**: Jesus redefined greatness, associating it with humility and service rather than power and status.

- **Model of Service**: He presented Himself as the ultimate example of a servant leader, emphasizing His mission to serve and sacrifice for others.

2. The Washing of the Disciples' Feet

One of the most powerful demonstrations of servant leadership is when Jesus washed His disciples' feet.

- **John 13:1-17**: Jesus washed the feet of His disciples, an act typically performed by the lowest servant in a household.

  - **Humility and Service**: By performing this humble act, Jesus demonstrated that no task is beneath a true leader. He showed that leaders should serve those they lead, regardless of their status.

  - **Instruction to Follow**: After washing their feet, Jesus instructed His disciples to follow His example, emphasizing that they should serve one another with the same humility and love.

3. Core Principles of Servant Leadership

Several core principles define servant leadership, many of which can be drawn directly from Jesus' teachings and actions.

- **Listening**: A servant leader listens intently to the needs and concerns of others. Jesus frequently listened to those around Him, understanding their needs before responding.

- **Empathy**: Servant leaders show empathy, understanding, and compassion towards others. Jesus consistently showed empathy, whether healing the sick, comforting the grieving, or forgiving sinners.

- **Healing**: Servant leadership involves helping others heal, both physically and emotionally. Jesus' ministry was marked by acts of healing and restoration.

- **Awareness**: Being aware of oneself and others is crucial for servant leaders. Jesus was always aware of His surroundings, the needs of the people, and the larger purpose of His mission.

- **Persuasion**: Rather than using authority to compel, servant leaders use persuasion and gentle guidance. Jesus often used parables and gentle persuasion to teach and inspire.

- **Conceptualization**: Servant leaders have the

ability to look beyond day-to-day realities and envision the greater purpose and goals. Jesus constantly pointed to the Kingdom of God and the bigger picture of God's plan.

- **Foresight**: This involves understanding lessons from the past, the realities of the present, and the likely outcomes of future decisions. Jesus demonstrated foresight, preparing His disciples for the challenges ahead.

- **Stewardship**: Servant leaders take responsibility for the well-being of others and the resources they manage. Jesus taught stewardship through parables such as the Parable of the Talents.

- **Commitment to the Growth of People**: Servant leaders are committed to the personal and professional growth of those they lead. Jesus invested in His disciples, teaching and mentoring them.

- **Building Community**: Creating a sense of community and belonging is a key aspect of servant leadership. Jesus built a community of followers, fostering a sense of unity and purpose.

4. Applications of Servant Leadership in Modern Contexts

Servant leadership is not just a biblical concept; it has practical applications in various modern contexts, including business, education, and community leadership.

- **Business**: In the corporate world, servant leaders prioritize the well-being and development of their employees. Companies with servant leaders often have higher employee satisfaction, better teamwork, and more ethical cultures.

  - **Example**: CEOs who practice servant leadership focus on empowering their teams, fostering a collaborative culture, and prioritizing employee development over short-term gains.

- **Education**: Teachers and school administrators can adopt servant leadership by focusing on the holistic development of their students and staff. This approach can lead to more supportive and effective learning environments.

  - **Example**: Principals who practice servant leadership actively support their teachers, encourage professional development, and create a positive school culture.

- **Community Leadership**: Community leaders who embody servant leadership work to better their communities by addressing the needs of

their members and fostering inclusive and supportive environments.

  ○ **Example**: Local government officials or non-
    profit leaders who focus on serving their com-
    munity's needs, promoting equity, and build-
    ing strong community ties.

5. Challenges and Misconceptions

While servant leadership is highly effective, it has challenges and misconceptions.

- **Perceived Weakness**: Some may perceive servant
  leaders as weak or lacking authority. However,
  servant leadership requires a strong commitment
  to values and the courage to prioritize others'
  needs.

- **Balance**: Servant leaders must balance serving
  others with making difficult decisions and providing direction. Effective servant leadership involves knowing when to be collaborative and
  when to take decisive action.

- **Sustainability**: Constantly serving others can
  lead to burnout if leaders do not also take care
  of their own well-being. Servant leaders need to
  practice self-care and delegate responsibilities to
  maintain their effectiveness.

6. Biblical Examples of Servant Leadership

In addition to Jesus, the Bible provides other examples of servant leadership.

- **Moses**: Despite his initial reluctance, Moses led the Israelites out of Egypt, often interceding on their behalf with God and serving their needs throughout their journey.

- **David**: Despite his flaws, King David demonstrated servant leadership by caring for his people and seeking God's guidance in his leadership.

- **Paul**: The Apostle Paul served the early Christian communities, often at great personal cost, focusing on their spiritual growth and well-being.

Integrity and Accountability

Integrity and accountability are essential components of ethical leadership. These principles are crucial for building trust, fostering a positive environment, and ensuring that leaders act in a manner consistent with their values and responsibilities. Jesus' teachings and actions provide a clear framework for understanding and implementing integrity and accountability in leadership.

1. Defining Integrity

Integrity involves adhering to moral and ethical principles, being honest, and maintaining consistency between one's actions and values. It is about doing the right thing, even when no one is watching.

- **Honesty and Transparency**: Integrity requires honesty and transparency in all dealings. Jesus emphasized the importance of truthfulness, as seen in His teaching, "Let your 'Yes' be 'Yes,' and your 'No,' 'No'" (Matthew 5:37). This means being straightforward and truthful, avoiding deceit and duplicity.

- **Consistency and Reliability**: A leader with integrity is consistent and reliable. Their actions align with their words, and they can be counted on to follow through on their commitments. This builds trust and credibility among followers.

2. The Importance of Accountability

Accountability involves being answerable for one's actions and decisions and accepting responsibility for the outcomes. It ensures that leaders are held to their commitments and standards.

- **Responsibility and Ownership**: Accountability means taking responsibility for both successes and failures. Leaders must own their decisions and their consequences, learning from mistakes and striving for continuous improvement.

- **Answerability to Others**: Leaders are accountable to those they lead and to higher authorities or governing bodies. This accountability helps prevent abuse of power and ensures that leaders act in the best interests of their followers.

3. Biblical Foundations of Integrity and Accountability

The Bible provides numerous examples and teachings on the importance of integrity and accountability.

- **Jesus and Integrity**: Jesus is the ultimate model of integrity. He lived a life consistent with His teachings, exemplifying honesty, humility, and moral uprightness. His integrity was evident when He resisted temptation in the wilderness (Matthew 4:1-11) and when He consistently acted in accordance with God's will.

- **Parable of the Talents**: In the Parable of the Talents (Matthew 25:14-30), Jesus emphasizes accountability. The servants are held accountable for how they used the resources entrusted to them. This parable teaches that we are responsible for how we utilize our gifts and opportunities.

4. Practical Aspects of Integrity and Accountability

Implementing integrity and accountability in leadership involves several practical steps.

- **Setting Clear Values and Standards**: Leaders should establish clear ethical standards and values that guide their actions and effectively communicate these standards to their followers.

- **Leading by Example**: Leaders must model the behavior they expect from others. This involves demonstrating honesty, reliability, and ethical conduct in all situations.

- **Encouraging Open Communication**: Creating an environment where followers feel comfortable raising concerns and providing feedback is essential. This openness fosters accountability and helps identify areas for improvement.

- **Regular Self-Assessment**: Leaders should regularly assess their actions and decisions against their ethical standards. This self-reflection helps maintain integrity and identify areas for growth.

- **Establishing Accountability Mechanisms**: Implementing systems such as performance reviews, audits, and transparency measures ensures that leaders are held accountable for their actions.

5. Challenges and Obstacles

Maintaining integrity and accountability can be challenging, especially in complex and high-pressure environments.

- **Temptation and Corruption**: Leaders may face temptations to compromise their integrity for personal gain or to avoid difficult consequences.

Resisting these temptations requires strong moral conviction and support from others.

- **Peer Pressure and Cultural Norms**: Leaders may encounter peer pressure or cultural norms that conflict with their ethical standards. Standing firm in their principles can be difficult but is essential for maintaining integrity.

- **Fear of Repercussions**: Fear of negative repercussions can deter leaders from taking responsibility for their actions. Overcoming this fear involves fostering a culture of forgiveness and learning rather than punishment.

6. Benefits of Integrity and Accountability

Leaders who prioritize integrity and accountability foster a positive and ethical environment, leading to several benefits.

- **Building Trust**: Integrity and accountability build trust among followers. When leaders are honest and accountable, they earn the respect and loyalty of those they lead.

- **Promoting Ethical Behavior**: Leaders who model integrity and accountability inspire others to follow suit, creating an ethical culture within the organization.

- **Enhancing Decision-Making**: Ethical leaders make decisions that are not only effective but also morally sound, leading to sustainable success.

- **Strengthening Reputation**: Organizations led by individuals with strong integrity and accountability are viewed more favorably, enhancing their reputation and credibility.

Conclusion

Servant Leadership

Servant leadership, as exemplified by Jesus, is a powerful and transformative approach to leadership. By prioritizing the needs and growth of those they lead, servant leaders foster trust, collaboration, and a sense of community. Jesus' teachings and actions, such as washing His disciples' feet and emphasizing the importance of humility and service, provide a clear model for this leadership style. In modern contexts, servant leadership can be applied effectively in business, education, and community settings, promoting a culture of empathy, support, and ethical behavior. By embracing servant leadership, leaders can create environments where everyone feels valued and empowered, leading to stronger, more cohesive, and more productive communities.

Integrity and Accountability

Integrity and accountability are crucial for ethical leadership, ensuring that leaders act consistently with their values and responsibilities. These principles build trust, promote ethical behavior, and enhance decision-making. Jesus' life and teachings provide a robust framework for understanding and practicing integrity and accountability. Leaders who model these qualities create a positive and transparent environment, encouraging others to follow their example. Despite the challenges, maintaining integrity and accountability leads to numerous benefits, including strengthened relationships, improved reputation, and sustainable success. Reflecting on these principles helps leaders grow and align their actions with ethical standards, fostering a culture of trust and respect.

Reflection Questions

Reflecting on the principles of servant leadership, and integrity and accountability, can help deepen understanding and application of these concepts. Here are some questions for reflection:

Servant Leadership

1. **Self-Assessment**: In what ways do you currently serve those you lead? How can you enhance your servant leadership practices?

2. **Humility**: Are there tasks or responsibilities you consider beneath you? How can you adopt a more humble approach in your leadership?

3. **Empathy**: How well do you listen to and understand the needs and concerns of those you lead?

What steps can you take to improve your empathy and responsiveness?

4. **Building Community**: How do you foster a sense of community and collaboration within your team or organization? What strategies can you implement to strengthen these bonds?

Integrity and Accountability

1. **Ethical Standards**: What ethical standards guide your decisions and actions? Are there areas where you struggle to maintain these standards?

2. **Honesty and Transparency**: How transparent are you with your team about your decisions and their reasons? How can you increase your transparency?

3. **Responsibility**: How do you handle mistakes or failures? Do you take responsibility and learn from them, or do you tend to deflect blame?

4. **Feedback and Improvement**: How open are you to receiving feedback from others? What steps can you take to create an environment where feedback is encouraged and valued?

By contemplating these questions, leaders can better understand and apply the principles of servant leadership, integrity, and accountability, fostering a more ethical and effective leadership approach.

Economic Justice and Fairness

Caring for the Poor and Responsible Stewardship

Caring for the Poor

Caring for the poor is a central theme in Jesus' teachings and an essential aspect of Christian discipleship. Jesus consistently demonstrated compassion for the poor and marginalized, urging His followers to do the same. Let's delve into the subtopic of caring for the poor, exploring its significance, practical implications, and the teachings of Jesus that underscore its importance.

1. Biblical Foundation

Jesus' teachings and actions provide a strong biblical foundation for caring for the poor.

- **The Sermon on the Mount**: In the Beatitudes, Jesus says, "Blessed are the poor in spirit, for theirs is the kingdom of heaven" (Matthew 5:3). This statement highlights God's special concern for the poor and His promise of spiritual blessings.

- **The Parable of the Sheep and the Goats**: In Matthew 25:31-46, Jesus describes the final judgment, where He separates people like a shepherd separates sheep from goats. He says to the righteous, "For I was hungry and you gave me something to eat, I was thirsty and you gave me something to drink... Truly I tell you, whatever you did for one of the least of these brothers and sisters of mine, you did for me." This parable emphasizes that serving the poor is equivalent to serving Jesus Himself.

- **Jesus' Mission Statement**: In Luke 4:18-19, Jesus reads from the scroll of Isaiah in the synagogue: "The Spirit of the Lord is on me, because he has anointed me to proclaim good news to the poor. He has sent me to proclaim freedom for the prisoners and recovery of sight for the blind, to set the oppressed free, to proclaim the year of the Lord's favor." This declaration outlines Jesus' mission, highlighting His commitment to the poor and oppressed.

2. Practical Implications

Caring for the poor involves more than just feelings of compassion; it requires concrete actions and systemic changes.

- **Providing Basic Needs**: Ensuring that the poor have access to basic necessities such as food, clothing, and shelter is a fundamental aspect of caring for them. This can be done through direct aid, community support programs, and charitable organizations.

- **Empowering the Poor**: Helping the poor involves empowering them to improve their circumstances. This can include providing education, job training, and resources that enable them to become self-sufficient.

- **Advocating for Social Justice**: Addressing the root causes of poverty often requires advocating for social justice. This might involve campaigning for fair wages, affordable housing, healthcare access, and policies that reduce economic inequality.

3. Jesus' Interactions with the Poor

Jesus' interactions with the poor and marginalized demonstrate His deep compassion and commitment to their well-being.

- **Healing the Sick and Disabled**: Jesus often healed those who were sick or disabled, many of whom were also poor and marginalized. For example, in Mark 10:46-52, Jesus heals Bartimaeus, a blind beggar. By restoring his sight, Jesus healed Bartimaeus physically and restored his dignity and place in society.

- **Feeding the Hungry**: Jesus performed miracles to feed the hungry, such as the feeding of the 5,000 (Matthew 14:13-21). This miracle illustrates His concern for the physical needs of the people and His willingness to provide for them.

- **Parables of Compassion**: Jesus used parables to teach about compassion for the poor. In the Parable of the Good Samaritan (Luke 10:25-37), He highlights the importance of showing mercy and caring for those in need, regardless of their background or social status.

4. The Early Church's Example

The early Christian community modeled Jesus' teachings by actively caring for the poor.

- **Community Sharing**: Acts 2:44-45 describes how the early believers shared everything in common: "All the believers were together and had everything in common. They sold property and possessions to give to anyone who had need." This communal living ensured that no one among them was in need.

- **Organized Support**: The early church organized support for the poor, such as the distribution of food. In Acts 6:1-7, the apostles appointed seven deacons to oversee the daily distribution of food to widows, ensuring that the vulnerable were cared for fairly.

5. Contemporary Applications

Jesus' teachings on caring for the poor have significant implications for contemporary society.

- **Charitable Organizations**: Many Christian and secular organizations are dedicated to alleviating poverty. Supporting these organizations through donations, volunteering, or advocacy is a practical way to care for the poor.

- **Personal Responsibility**: Individuals are called to reflect Jesus' compassion in their own lives. This can involve simple acts of kindness, such as providing meals to the homeless, supporting local food banks, or helping a needy neighbor.

- **Policy Advocacy**: Christians can also engage in advocacy to influence policies that address the systemic causes of poverty. This might involve lobbying for living wages, healthcare reform, affordable housing, and education access.

6. Challenges and Obstacles

Caring for the poor can be challenging and requires overcoming various obstacles.

- **Economic Inequality**: The vast gap between the rich and the poor poses a significant challenge. Addressing this inequality requires systemic changes and collective effort.

- **Stigmatization**: The poor are often stigmatized and blamed for their circumstances. Combating these prejudices and promoting a more compassionate perspective is essential.

- **Sustainable Solutions**: Providing immediate relief is important, but sustainable solutions are necessary to address the root causes of poverty. This involves long-term strategies and investment in education, infrastructure, and economic opportunities.

Responsible Stewardship

Responsible stewardship is a key aspect of economic justice and fairness, emphasizing the careful and responsible management of resources, talents, and opportunities entrusted to individuals. Jesus' teachings provide profound insights into stewardship principles, highlighting accountability, diligence, and the ethical use of resources.

1. Biblical Foundation of Stewardship

Jesus' teachings include parables and statements that underscore the importance of responsible stewardship.

- **The Parable of the Talents**: In Matthew 25:14-30, Jesus tells the Parable of the Talents, where a master entrusts his servants with varying amounts of money. The servants who invest and grow their master's money are praised, while the one who buries his talent out of fear is rebuked.

This parable illustrates the importance of using one's resources and abilities wisely and productively.

- **Faithful Stewardship**: In Luke 12:42-48, Jesus speaks about the faithful and wise manager who is put in charge of the master's servants. He emphasizes that to whom much is given, much will be required, highlighting the responsibility that comes with stewardship.

2. Principles of Responsible Stewardship

Several principles can be drawn from Jesus' teachings on stewardship.

- **Accountability**: Stewards are accountable to God and others for how they manage their resources. This involves transparency and integrity in all dealings.

- **Diligence and Hard Work**: Responsible stewardship requires diligence and hard work. In the Parable of the Talents, Jesus commended the diligent servants and criticized laziness and complacency.

- **Wise Management**: Stewards must manage resources wisely, making prudent decisions that maximize their value and impact. This includes financial stewardship, time management, and the ethical use of talents and skills.

- **Generosity and Compassion**: True stewardship involves using resources not just for personal gain but for the benefit of others. Jesus taught generosity, emphasizing the importance of caring for the poor and supporting the community.

3. Stewardship of Material Resources

Jesus' teachings encourage the responsible management of material resources.

- **Avoiding Greed**: In Luke 12:15, Jesus warns, "Watch out! Be on your guard against all kinds of greed; life does not consist in an abundance of possessions." Responsible stewardship involves avoiding greed and the excessive accumulation of wealth.

- **Helping Those in Need**: In Matthew 6:19-21, Jesus advises storing up treasures in heaven rather than on earth, emphasizing the eternal value of generosity. Using material resources to help those in need aligns with responsible stewardship.

4. Stewardship of Talents and Abilities

Jesus encourages the responsible use of personal talents and abilities.

- **Using Gifts Wisely**: The Parable of the Talents (Matthew 25:14-30) underscores the importance of productively using one's abilities. Each person is given different gifts and opportunities and is expected to use them wisely for the greater good.

- **Developing Skills**: Responsible stewardship involves continually developing and improving one's skills and abilities to serve God and others better. This commitment to personal growth reflects diligent stewardship.

5. Stewardship of Time

Time is a valuable resource that must be managed wisely.

- **Prioritizing God's Kingdom**: In Matthew 6:33, Jesus says, "But seek first his kingdom and his righteousness, and all these things will be given to you as well." Responsible stewardship of time involves prioritizing spiritual growth, worship, and service to others.

- **Balancing Responsibilities**: Stewardship requires balancing various responsibilities, ensuring that time is allocated effectively to work, rest, family, and community service.

6. Environmental Stewardship

Caring for the environment is a form of responsible stewardship.

- **Creation Care**: While Jesus did not explicitly address environmental issues, His teachings on stewardship can be applied to caring for the earth. Genesis 2:15 emphasizes humanity's responsibility to "work it and take care of" the Garden of Eden, suggesting that environmental stewardship is a biblical mandate.

- **Sustainable Practices**: Responsible stewardship involves adopting sustainable practices that protect and preserve the environment for future generations. This includes reducing waste, conserving resources, and supporting ecological initiatives.

7. Challenges of Responsible Stewardship

Implementing responsible stewardship can be challenging but is essential for ethical living.

- **Materialism**: In a consumer-driven society, resisting materialism and prioritizing responsible stewardship requires intentional effort and spiritual discipline.

- **Ethical Dilemmas**: Navigating ethical dilemmas in resource management, such as fair trade, labor practices, and environmental impact, requires wisdom and commitment to biblical principles.

Conclusion

Caring for the Poor

Caring for the poor is a fundamental aspect of Jesus' teachings, reflecting His deep compassion and commitment to social justice. Through His parables, actions, and direct instructions, Jesus emphasized the importance of providing for those in need, empowering the marginalized, and advocating for social justice. By following His example, individuals and communities can work towards alleviating poverty and creating a more just and compassionate society.

Responsible Stewardship

Responsible stewardship is a vital principle in Jesus' teachings, emphasizing the ethical and productive use of resources, talents, and time. Jesus' parables and statements underscore the importance of accountability, diligence, and generosity in managing what has been entrusted to us. By practicing responsible stewardship, individuals can honor God, benefit others, and contribute to the flourishing of their communities and the world.

Reflection Questions

Caring for the Poor

1. **Awareness**: Who are the poor and marginalized in your community, and how can you become more aware of their needs and challenges?

2. **Action**: What practical steps can you take to provide for the basic needs of the poor, such as food, clothing, and shelter?

3. **Empowerment**: How can you contribute to empowering the poor, helping them achieve self-sufficiency through education, job training, and other resources?

4. **Advocacy**: What social justice issues are you passionate about, and how can you advocate for policies that address the root causes of poverty and inequality?

5. **Personal Responsibility**: In what ways can you integrate Jesus' teachings on caring for the poor into your daily life and interactions with others?

Responsible Stewardship

1. **Resource Management**: How can you responsibly manage your material resources, avoiding

greed and prioritizing generosity?

2. **Using Talents**: What talents and abilities have been entrusted to you, and how can you use them productively for the benefit of others and the glory of God?

3. **Time Management**: How do you currently manage your time, and what changes can you make to prioritize spiritual growth, service, and balanced living?

4. **Environmental Care**: What steps can you take to practice environmental stewardship, adopting sustainable habits that protect and preserve the earth?

5. **Overcoming Challenges**: What challenges do you face in practicing responsible stewardship, and how can you address them through prayer, accountability, and commitment to biblical principles?

Reflecting on these questions can help individuals understand and apply the principles of caring for the poor and responsible stewardship in their daily lives, fostering a more just, compassionate, and ethical world.

Mental and Emotional Well-being

Peace and Inner Calm

Peace and Inner Calm

Peace and inner calm are essential for mental and emotional well-being. Jesus' teachings provide profound guidance on how to achieve and maintain inner peace despite the challenges and stresses of life. By exploring His sayings and actions, we can gain a deeper understanding of how to cultivate peace and tranquility in our own lives.

1. Jesus' Promise of Peace

Jesus promised His followers peace, a peace that is different from what the world offers.

- **John 14:27**: "Peace I leave with you; my peace I give you. I do not give to you as the world gives. Do not let your hearts be troubled and do not be afraid."

  - **Divine Peace**: Jesus offers a peace that transcends worldly understanding, a deep and abiding sense of calm that comes from trust in God.

- ○ **Freedom from Fear**: This peace helps to calm our fears and anxieties, providing a foundation of stability and security.

2. Peace in the Midst of Turmoil

Jesus demonstrated that it is possible to have peace even in the midst of chaos and turmoil.

- **Mark 4:35-41**: The story of Jesus calming the storm illustrates His authority over nature and His ability to bring peace in chaotic situations. When the disciples were terrified, Jesus rebuked the wind and said to the waves, "Quiet! Be still!" The wind died down, and it was completely calm.

  - ○ **Trust in Jesus**: This event teaches us to trust in Jesus during life's storms, knowing that He has the power to bring calm and peace.

  - ○ **Inner Calm**: Even when external circumstances are turbulent, we can find inner calm by focusing on Jesus and His promises.

3. Peace through Prayer

Jesus taught and practiced prayer as a way to connect with God and find peace.

- **Philippians 4:6-7**: Paul, echoing Jesus' teachings, writes, "Do not be anxious about anything, but in every situation, by prayer and petition, with thanksgiving, present your requests to God. And the peace of God, which transcends all understanding, will guard your hearts and your minds in Christ Jesus."

- ○ **Relieving Anxiety**: Prayer is a powerful tool for relieving anxiety and stress, allowing us to place our burdens in God's hands.

- ○ **Guarding Hearts and Minds**: The peace that comes through prayer acts as a guard over our hearts and minds, protecting us from worry and fear.

4. Jesus as the Prince of Peace

Jesus is often referred to as the "Prince of Peace," emphasizing His role in bringing peace to humanity.

- **Isaiah 9:6**: "For to us a child is born, to us a son is given, and the government will be on his shoulders. And he will be called Wonderful Counselor, Mighty God, Everlasting Father, Prince of Peace."

  - ○ **Peace through Relationship**: By establishing a relationship with Jesus, we can experience the peace that He brings.

  - ○ **Eternal Peace**: Jesus offers not just temporary relief but an eternal peace that comes from reconciliation with God.

5. The Beatitudes and Peacemaking

Jesus highlighted the importance of peacemaking as a blessed and virtuous pursuit.

- **Matthew 5:9**: "Blessed are the peacemakers, for they will be called children of God."

  ○ **Active Peacemaking**: Being a peacemaker involves actively promoting peace and reconciliation in our relationships and communities.

  ○ **Identity as God's Children**: Peacemakers reflect the character of God and are recognized as His children, contributing to inner calm through living out their faith.

6. Overcoming Worry

Jesus specifically addressed worry and provided guidance on how to overcome it to find peace.

- **Matthew 6:25-34**: In the Sermon on the Mount, Jesus tells His followers not to worry about their lives, what they will eat or drink, or about their bodies, what they will wear. He assures them that God knows their needs and will provide.

  ○ **Trust in Provision**: Trusting in God's provision helps alleviate worry and fosters a sense of peace.

- **Focus on the Present**: Jesus encourages focusing on the present rather than worrying about the future, which can help reduce anxiety and bring inner calm.

7. Forgiveness and Reconciliation

Forgiving others and seeking reconciliation are essential for inner peace.

- **Matthew 6:14-15**: "For if you forgive other people when they sin against you, your heavenly Father will also forgive you. But if you do not forgive others their sins, your Father will not forgive your sins."

  - **Healing Relationships**: Forgiveness helps heal broken relationships and remove the burden of resentment, leading to peace.

  - **Spiritual Peace**: By forgiving others, we align ourselves with God's will and receive His forgiveness, contributing to spiritual and emotional peace.

8. Living in Harmony

Jesus' teachings encourage living in harmony with others as a path to peace.

- **Romans 12:18**: Paul, drawing from Jesus' teachings, advises, "If it is possible, as far as it depends on you, live at peace with everyone."

- ○ **Effort towards Peace**: Striving to live at peace with others involves humility, patience, and understanding, all of which contribute to inner calm.

- ○ **Community Peace**: Peace within communities fosters a supportive environment, reducing stress and anxiety.

9. Jesus' Post-Resurrection Appearances

After His resurrection, Jesus greeted His disciples with words of peace, reinforcing His role as the giver of peace.
- **John 20:19-21**: "On the evening of that first day of the week, when the disciples were together, with the doors locked for fear of the Jewish leaders, Jesus came and stood among them and said, 'Peace be with you!'"

  - ○ **Reassurance and Comfort**: Jesus' greeting of peace reassured and comforted His disciples, who were fearful and uncertain.

  - ○ **Presence of Jesus**: The presence of Jesus brought peace to His followers, reminding us that His presence in our lives can also bring us peace.

10. Meditation on Jesus' Words

Meditating on Jesus' teachings and His words can bring peace and inner calm.

- **John 15:4**: "Remain in me, as I also remain in you. No branch can bear fruit by itself; it must remain in the vine. Neither can you bear fruit unless you remain in me."

  - **Abiding in Christ**: Maintaining a close relationship with Jesus through meditation and prayer fosters a sense of peace and inner calm.

  - **Spiritual Nourishment**: Staying connected to Jesus, like a branch to a vine, provides spiritual nourishment that strengthens our inner peace.

Overcoming Worry

Overcoming worry is crucial for maintaining mental and emotional well-being. Jesus addressed worry directly in His teachings, providing insights and guidance on how to live a worry-free life. We can find peace and trust in God's provision and care by understanding and applying these principles.

1. Jesus' Teaching on Worry

In the Sermon on the Mount, Jesus provides a comprehensive teaching on overcoming worry.

- **Matthew 6:25-34**: Jesus says, "Therefore I tell you, do not worry about your life, what you will eat or drink; or about your body, what you will wear. Is not life more than food, and the body more than clothes? Look at the birds of the air; they do not sow or reap or store away in barns, and yet your heavenly Father feeds them. Are you not much more valuable than they? Can any one of you by worrying add a single hour to your life?"

    - **Trust in God's Provision**: Jesus emphasizes that God provides for the birds and the flowers, and He will surely provide for us. This teaching encourages us to trust in God's care and provision.

    - **Value and Worth**: Jesus reassures us of our value to God, implying that if He cares for the lesser creations, He will certainly care for us.

2. Focusing on Today

Jesus teaches the importance of focusing on the present rather than worrying about the future.

- **Matthew 6:34**: "Therefore do not worry about tomorrow, for tomorrow will worry about itself.

Each day has enough trouble of its own."

- ○ **Living in the Present**: Jesus advises us to focus on today and handle the challenges of the present moment. This helps reduce anxiety about the future and fosters a sense of peace.

- ○ **Day-by-Day Approach**: By taking life one day at a time, we can manage stress more effectively and remain grounded in the present.

3. Seeking First the Kingdom of God

Jesus provides a priority for life that helps alleviate worry.
- **Matthew 6:33**: "But seek first his kingdom and his righteousness, and all these things will be given to you as well."

- ○ **Prioritizing Spiritual Goals**: By focusing on God's kingdom and His righteousness, we align our priorities with God's will. This shift in focus can help reduce worry about material needs and concerns.

- ○ **Promise of Provision**: Jesus promises that when we prioritize God's kingdom, our material needs will be taken care of, reducing the stress and anxiety related to these concerns.

4. Faith and Trust in God

Faith and trust in God are central to overcoming worry.

- **Matthew 6:30**: "If that is how God clothes the grass of the field, which is here today and tomorrow is thrown into the fire, will he not much more clothe you—you of little faith?"

  - **Building Faith**: Jesus highlights that worry often stems from a lack of faith. Strengthening our faith and trust in God's provision helps to alleviate worry.

  - **God's Faithfulness**: Reflecting on God's faithfulness in the past can build our trust in His continued care and provision.

5. Jesus' Example of Prayer

Jesus demonstrated the importance of prayer in overcoming worry.

- **Luke 22:39-46**: In the Garden of Gethsemane, Jesus prayed earnestly before His crucifixion. Despite His anguish, He ultimately submitted to God's will, saying, "Father, if you are willing, take this cup from me; yet not my will, but yours be done."

  - **Seeking God's Will**: Prayer helps us align with God's will and find peace in His plan, even when facing difficult circumstances.

- ○ **Relief through Prayer**: Jesus' example shows that prayer is a powerful tool for overcoming worry and finding strength and peace in God.

6. Avoiding Materialism

Jesus warns against the pursuit of material wealth, which can be a source of worry.

- • **Matthew 6:19-21**: "Do not store up for yourselves treasures on earth, where moths and vermin destroy, and where thieves break in and steal. But store up for yourselves treasures in heaven, where moths and vermin do not destroy, and where thieves do not break in and steal. For where your treasure is, there your heart will be also."

  - ○ **Eternal Perspective**: Focusing on spiritual wealth rather than material wealth reduces worry about earthly possessions.

  - ○ **Heart Alignment**: By aligning our hearts with eternal values, we can diminish the anxiety that comes from pursuing temporary and materialistic goals.

7. Living in God's Peace

Jesus invites us to live in His peace, which is a powerful antidote to worry.

- **John 14:27**: "Peace I leave with you; my peace I give you. I do not give to you as the world gives. Do not let your hearts be troubled and do not be afraid."

  - **Receiving Jesus' Peace**: Embracing the peace that Jesus offers helps to calm our hearts and minds, providing a sense of tranquility that counteracts worry.

  - **Different Kind of Peace**: Jesus' peace is not dependent on circumstances but is a deep, abiding peace that comes from a relationship with Him.

8. Encouragement to Support Each Other

Supporting one another in faith can help alleviate worry.
- **Galatians 6:2**: "Carry each other's burdens, and in this way you will fulfill the law of Christ."

  - **Community Support**: Sharing our concerns with others and supporting each other can provide comfort and reduce the burden of worry.

  - **Fulfilling Christ's Law**: By helping one another, we live out Jesus' command to love and support each other, fostering a supportive community.

Conclusion

Peace and Inner Calm

Peace and inner calm are vital for mental and emotional well-being. Jesus' teachings offer profound guidance on how to achieve and maintain peace. By trusting in His promises, focusing on the present, and prioritizing spiritual goals, we can experience the deep, abiding peace that Jesus offers. Through prayer, forgiveness, and living harmoniously with others, we cultivate inner calm, enabling us to navigate life's challenges with tranquility and confidence.

Overcoming Worry

Overcoming worry is essential for maintaining mental and emotional health. Jesus' teachings provide practical strategies for addressing worry, including trusting in God's provision, living in the present, seeking God's kingdom first, and relying on prayer. By building our faith and focusing on spiritual priorities, we can reduce anxiety and embrace the peace that Jesus offers. Supporting one another and avoiding materialism further helps to alleviate worry, allowing us to live more fulfilled and peaceful lives.

Reflection Questions

Peace and Inner Calm

1. **Jesus' Promise**: How can you more fully embrace the peace that Jesus offers? What steps can you take to trust in His promise of peace?

2. **Handling Chaos**: How do you typically react to chaotic or stressful situations? How can you apply Jesus' example of calming the storm to find peace in your own life?

3. **Prayer**: How often do you turn to prayer when you feel anxious or troubled? What changes can you make to incorporate more prayer into your daily routine to cultivate peace?

4. **Peacemaking**: In what ways can you actively promote peace and reconciliation in your relationships and community?

Overcoming Worry

1. **Trust in Provision**: What specific worries do you need to trust God with? How can you remind yourself of God's faithfulness and provision in your daily life?

2. **Present Focus**: Are there areas in your life where

you are overly focused on the future? How can you practice focusing on the present to reduce anxiety?

3. **Seeking God's Kingdom**: How can you prioritize seeking God's kingdom in your daily activities and decisions?

4. **Prayer and Faith**: How does your prayer life help you manage worry? How can you strengthen your faith and trust in God's care?

5. **Materialism**: Are there aspects of materialism that contribute to worry in your life? How can you shift your focus from material possessions to spiritual values?

Reflecting on these questions can help individuals apply Jesus' teachings on peace, inner calm, and overcoming worry, fostering a more balanced and spiritually grounded life.

Environmental Stewardship

Caring for Creation

Caring for Creation

Caring for creation is an essential aspect of environmental stewardship, reflecting the biblical mandate to protect and preserve the Earth. While Jesus did not explicitly address environmental issues, His teachings, and the broader biblical context provide clear guidance on the importance of caring for the world God created. By understanding these principles, we can apply them to contemporary challenges and foster a sustainable relationship with the environment.

1. Biblical Mandate for Stewardship

The Bible provides a foundational mandate for environmental stewardship.

- **Genesis 2:15**: "The Lord God took the man and put him in the Garden of Eden to work it and take care of it."

    - **Role of Stewardship**: This verse highlights humanity's responsibility to "work" and "take care" of the Earth, implying active management and preservation of natural resources.

- ○ **Creation Care**: The task given to Adam signifies the importance of caring for creation as a divine mandate.

2. Jesus' Teachings on Stewardship

Although Jesus did not directly address environmental issues, His teachings on stewardship apply to caring for creation.

- **Parable of the Talents**: In Matthew 25:14-30, Jesus emphasizes the importance of wisely managing the resources entrusted to us. This principle extends to how we manage the Earth's resources, encouraging sustainable and responsible use.

- **Luke 12:42-48**: Jesus speaks about the faithful and wise manager who takes care of what is entrusted to him. This parable reinforces the concept of accountability and diligent stewardship.

3. Respect for God's Creation

Jesus' appreciation for nature reflects the value of creation.

- **Matthew 6:26-29**: "Look at the birds of the air; they do not sow or reap or store away in barns, and yet your heavenly Father feeds them. Are you not much more valuable than they? ... See how the flowers of the field grow. They do not labor or spin. Yet I tell you that not even Solomon in all his splendor was dressed like one of these."

- **God's Provision**: Jesus points to nature as evidence of God's provision and care, highlighting the intrinsic value of all creation.

- **Appreciation for Nature**: By acknowledging the beauty and provision in nature, Jesus encourages us to appreciate and respect the natural world.

4. Interconnectedness of Creation

Jesus' teachings reflect the interconnectedness of all creation.

- **Matthew 10:29-31**: "Are not two sparrows sold for a penny? Yet not one of them will fall to the ground outside your Father's care. And even the very hairs of your head are all numbered. So don't be afraid; you are worth more than many sparrows."

  - **Divine Care for All**: This passage emphasizes that God's care extends to all parts of creation, suggesting that every element of the natural world is important and interconnected.

  - **Human Responsibility**: Understanding this interconnectedness highlights our responsibility to care for all aspects of creation, recognizing that our actions impact the broader ecosystem.

5. Principles of Sustainable Living

Applying Jesus' teachings to modern environmental issues involves principles of sustainable living.

- **Reduce, Reuse, Recycle**: These principles align with the concept of wise stewardship, encouraging us to use resources responsibly and minimize waste.

  - **Resource Management**: Like the servants in the Parable of the Talents, we are called to manage our resources effectively, ensuring that we do not deplete or destroy them.

- **Conservation Efforts**: Efforts to conserve natural resources, such as water and energy, reflect responsible stewardship.

  - **Long-Term Thinking**: Sustainable living requires thinking beyond immediate needs and considering the long-term impact of our actions on the environment.

6. Combatting Environmental Degradation

Christians are called to combat environmental degradation as part of their stewardship responsibilities.

- **Pollution Reduction**: Reducing pollution,

whether air, water, or soil, is essential to preserving the environment.

- ○ **Clean Energy**: Investing in clean and renewable energy sources helps reduce our ecological footprint and protect the planet for future generations.

- **Biodiversity Protection**: Protecting biodiversity ensures the stability and resilience of ecosystems.

- ○ **Habitat Conservation**: Efforts to conserve habitats, such as forests and wetlands, are crucial for maintaining biodiversity and ecosystem health.

7. Community and Global Action

Environmental stewardship involves both individual and collective action.

- **Community Involvement**: Engaging in community efforts, such as local clean-up projects and conservation programs, helps foster a sense of shared responsibility.

- ○ **Education and Advocacy**: Educating others about environmental issues and advocating for sustainable policies contribute to broader societal change.

- **Global Perspective**: Christians can support international efforts to combat climate change and protect natural resources by acknowledging that environmental issues are global in scope.

- ○ **Solidarity and Justice**: Environmental justice involves addressing the disproportionate impact of environmental degradation on vulnerable communities.

Conclusion

Caring for creation is an integral part of our stewardship responsibilities, rooted in biblical principles and Jesus' teachings. By appreciating the value of nature, recognizing the interconnectedness of all creation, and applying principles of sustainable living, we can fulfill our divine mandate to protect and preserve the Earth. Combatting environmental degradation and engaging in community and global action are essential for ensuring a healthy and sustainable planet for future generations. Through these efforts, we honor God and reflect His care for all of creation.

Reflective Questions

1. **Biblical Mandate**: How does the biblical mandate to "work and take care of" the Earth influence your view of environmental stewardship? What practical steps can you take to fulfill this mandate?

2. **Appreciation for Nature**: How can you cultivate a greater appreciation for the natural world in your daily life? What specific actions can you take to show respect for God's creation?

3. **Sustainable Living**: In what ways can you incorporate the principles of reduce, reuse, and recycle into your lifestyle? How can you manage your resources more responsibly?

4. **Community Action**: What opportunities exist in your community for environmental stewardship? How can you get involved in local conservation efforts or educational programs?

5. **Global Perspective**: How can you support global efforts to combat climate change and protect natural resources? What role can advocacy and education play in promoting environmental justice?

Reflecting on these questions can help individuals understand and apply the principles of caring for creation, fostering a deeper commitment to environmental stewardship in their personal and community lives.

Community and Social Responsibility

Building Community and Active Citizenship

Building Community

Building a strong, supportive community is essential for fostering social responsibility and creating an environment where individuals can thrive. Jesus' teachings provide valuable insights into building and sustaining communities that reflect love, support, and mutual respect. By examining His words and actions, we can learn how to create communities that embody the principles of the Kingdom of God.

1. The Greatest Commandment

Jesus emphasized the importance of loving God and loving others as foundational to building a strong community.

- **Matthew 22:37-39**: Jesus replied, "Love the Lord your God with all your heart and with all your soul and with all your mind.' This is the first and greatest commandment. And the second is like it: 'Love your neighbor as yourself.'"

- **Foundation of Love**: Love for God and others forms the basis of a strong community. This love encourages respect, compassion, and a commitment to the well-being of all members.

- **Mutual Respect**: By loving our neighbors as ourselves, we cultivate a community where everyone feels valued and respected.

2. The Golden Rule

Jesus' teaching of the Golden Rule is a practical guide for building harmonious relationships within a community.

- **Matthew 7:12**: "So in everything, do to others what you would have them do to you, for this sums up the Law and the Prophets."

  - **Reciprocity and Empathy**: The Golden Rule encourages treating others with the same kindness and consideration we desire for ourselves, fostering empathy and mutual respect.

  - **Positive Interaction**: This principle promotes positive interactions and helps resolve conflicts, contributing to a peaceful and supportive community.

3. The Power of Forgiveness

Forgiveness is crucial for maintaining harmony and unity within a community.

- **Matthew 6:14-15**: "For if you forgive other people when they sin against you, your heavenly Father will also forgive you. But if you do not forgive others their sins, your Father will not forgive your sins."

  - **Healing Relationships**: Forgiveness helps heal broken relationships and prevents resentment from undermining community cohesion.

  - **Promoting Peace**: A community that practices forgiveness is more likely to experience peace and unity, as members are willing to move past conflicts and work together constructively.

4. Serving One Another

Jesus taught that serving others is a fundamental aspect of community life.

- **Mark 10:45**: "For even the Son of Man did not come to be served, but to serve, and to give his life as a ransom for many."

  - **Service and Humility**: Serving one another fosters humility and selflessness, essential qualities for building a supportive community.

  - **Strengthening Bonds**: Acts of service strengthen the bonds between community members, creating a sense of solidarity and mutual support.

5. Welcoming the Stranger

Inclusivity and hospitality are key to building a diverse and welcoming community.

- **Matthew 25:35**: "For I was hungry and you gave me something to eat, I was thirsty and you gave me something to drink, I was a stranger and you invited me in."

  - **Hospitality**: Welcoming strangers and providing for their needs demonstrates love and compassion, essential for a vibrant community.

  - **Inclusivity**: Embracing diversity and making newcomers feel welcome enriches the community and reflects the inclusive nature of God's Kingdom.

6. Encouraging One Another

Encouragement and support are vital for building a positive and uplifting community.

- **1 Thessalonians 5:11**: "Therefore encourage one another and build each other up, just as in fact you are doing."

  - **Positive Reinforcement**: Encouragement

helps individuals feel valued and motivated, contributing to their personal growth and well-being.

○ **Building Morale**: A community that actively encourages its members fosters a positive atmosphere and high morale.

7. Living in Harmony

Jesus' teachings emphasize the importance of living in harmony with others.

- **Romans 12:16**: "Live in harmony with one another. Do not be proud, but be willing to associate with people of low position. Do not be conceited."

  ○ **Humility and Unity**: Living in harmony involves humility, openness, and a willingness to connect with others, regardless of their social status.

  ○ **Conflict Resolution**: Harmony requires addressing conflicts constructively and striving for peaceful resolutions.

8. Sharing Resources

Sharing resources and helping those in need is a tangible way to build a caring community.

- **Acts 4:32-35**: "All the believers were one in heart

and mind. No one claimed that any of their possessions was their own, but they shared everything they had. With great power the apostles continued to testify to the resurrection of the Lord Jesus. And God's grace was so powerfully at work in them all that there were no needy persons among them."

- ◦ **Generosity**: Sharing resources ensures that the needs of all community members are met, fostering equality and mutual care.

- ◦ **Collective Responsibility**: This practice reflects a sense of collective responsibility and solidarity, strengthening the community.

9. Praying Together

Prayer unites community members spiritually and strengthens their collective faith.
- • **Matthew 18:20**: "For where two or three gather in my name, there am I with them."

  - ◦ **Spiritual Unity**: Praying together fosters spiritual unity and a sense of shared purpose.

  - ◦ **Divine Guidance**: Collective prayer seeks God's guidance and blessings for the community, reinforcing their faith and commitment.

10. Teaching and Discipleship

Teaching and discipleship are essential for nurturing spiritual growth within the community.

- **Matthew 28:19-20**: "Therefore go and make disciples of all nations, baptizing them in the name of the Father and of the Son and of the Holy Spirit, and teaching them to obey everything I have commanded you. And surely I am with you always, to the very end of the age."

  - **Education and Growth**: Teaching and discipleship help community members grow in their faith and understanding of Jesus' teachings.

  - **Shared Mission**: Engaging in discipleship fosters a shared mission and purpose, strengthening the community's unity and commitment to living out the gospel.

Active Citizenship

Active citizenship involves taking an engaged and proactive role in the community to promote the common good, justice, and equity. Jesus' teachings provide a rich framework for understanding and practicing active citizenship. By exploring His sayings and actions, we can learn how to contribute positively to our communities and society as a whole.

1. Being "Salt and Light"

Jesus calls His followers to be influential in the world, acting as agents of change and goodness.

- **Matthew 5:13-16**: "You are the salt of the earth. But if the salt loses its saltiness, how can it be made salty again? ... You are the light of the world. A town built on a hill cannot be hidden... In the same way, let your light shine before others, that they may see your good deeds and glorify your Father in heaven."

  - **Influence for Good**: Just as salt enhances flavor and preserves food, Christians are called to enhance and preserve the moral and ethical fabric of society.

  - **Visibility and Witness**: Being the light of the world means living visibly righteous lives that inspire and guide others toward goodness.

2. Advocating for Justice

Jesus demonstrated a profound commitment to justice and righteousness, challenging systems of oppression and advocating for the marginalized.

- **Luke 4:18-19**: "The Spirit of the Lord is on me, because he has anointed me to proclaim good news to the poor. He has sent me to proclaim freedom for the prisoners and recovery of sight for the blind, to set the oppressed free, to proclaim the year of the Lord's favor."

○ **Justice for the Oppressed**: Jesus' mission included advocating for the poor, the imprisoned, and the oppressed, setting an example for active citizenship focused on justice.

○ **Public Advocacy**: Christians are encouraged to speak out against injustice and work towards systems and policies that reflect God's righteousness.

3. Engaging in Civic Duties

Active citizenship involves fulfilling civic responsibilities such as voting, participating in public discourse, and contributing to community life.

• **Romans 13:1-7**: Paul teaches about the importance of respecting and submitting to governing authorities, which are instituted by God. This includes paying taxes and fulfilling civic obligations.

○ **Civic Responsibility**: Christians are called to be responsible citizens who engage in civic duties and respect lawful authorities.

○ **Participation in Governance**: Engaging in the political process, such as voting and advocacy, is a way to influence governance and promote justice and the common good.

4. Loving Your Neighbor

Active citizenship is rooted in the principle of loving one's neighbor and seeking their welfare.

- **Matthew 22:39**: "Love your neighbor as yourself."

  - **Community Welfare**: Active citizenship involves working for the community's welfare, addressing needs, and promoting well-being.

  - **Acts of Service**: Engaging in volunteer work, supporting local initiatives, and helping those in need are practical expressions of loving one's neighbor.

5. Peacemaking and Reconciliation

Promoting peace and reconciliation is a key aspect of active citizenship.

- **Matthew 5:9**: "Blessed are the peacemakers, for they will be called children of God."

  - **Conflict Resolution**: Active citizens work to resolve conflicts and foster reconciliation within their communities.

  - **Building Bridges**: Peacemaking involves building bridges between different groups, promoting understanding, and fostering harmonious relationships.

6. Stewardship of Resources

Managing resources wisely and ethically is part of active citizenship.

- **Luke 16:10**: "Whoever can be trusted with very little can also be trusted with much, and whoever is dishonest with very little will also be dishonest with much."

  - **Ethical Stewardship**: Active citizens are called to responsibly manage personal, communal, and environmental resources.

  - **Supporting Sustainable Practices**: Promoting and engaging in sustainable practices ensures that resources are used wisely and preserved for future generations.

7. Promoting Education and Awareness

Active citizenship includes promoting education and raising awareness about important social issues.

- **Hosea 4:6**: "My people are destroyed from lack of knowledge."

  - **Informed Participation**: Educating oneself and others about social issues is crucial for effective participation in civic life.

  - **Advocacy and Awareness**: Raising awareness and advocating for education and informed decision-making contribute to a knowledgeable and engaged community.

8. Compassion and Empathy

Practicing compassion and empathy is essential for active citizenship.

- **Matthew 25:35-40**: Jesus speaks about caring for the least among us, "For I was hungry and you gave me something to eat, I was thirsty and you gave me something to drink..."

  - **Compassionate Action**: Active citizens respond to the needs of the vulnerable and marginalized with compassion and empathy.

  - **Inclusive Community**: Ensuring that all members of the community are treated with dignity and respect fosters an inclusive and supportive society.

9. Building Strong Relationships

Active citizenship involves building strong, supportive relationships within the community.

- **John 13:34-35**: "A new command I give you: Love one another. As I have loved you, so you must love one another. By this everyone will know that you are my disciples, if you love one another."

- **Mutual Support**: Building strong relationships based on love and mutual support strengthens the fabric of the community.

- **Collective Strength**: A community united in love and support is more resilient and effective in addressing common challenges.

Conclusion

Building Community

Building a strong community rooted in love, respect, and mutual support is essential for fostering a sense of belonging and collective well-being. Jesus' teachings emphasize the importance of love, service, forgiveness, and inclusivity as foundational principles for creating harmonious and supportive communities. By actively practicing these principles, individuals can contribute to building communities that reflect the values of the Kingdom of God, where everyone is valued and cared for.

Active Citizenship

Active citizenship involves taking an engaged and proactive role in the community to promote justice, peace, and the common good. Jesus' teachings provide a rich framework for understanding and practicing active citizenship, emphasizing the importance of being "salt and light," advocating for justice, fulfilling civic responsibilities, and loving one's neighbor. By embodying these principles, individuals can make meaningful contributions to their communities and society, promoting a just and compassionate world.

Reflective Questions

Building Community

1. **Love and Respect**: How can you actively demonstrate love and respect for your neighbors within your community? What steps can you take to ensure that everyone feels valued and included?

2. **Service**: In what ways can you serve others in your community more effectively? What opportunities exist for you to contribute your time and talents to support those in need?

3. **Forgiveness**: Are there any relationships within your community that need healing through forgiveness? How can you initiate the process of forgiveness and reconciliation?

4. **Inclusivity**: How can you make newcomers feel welcome and included in your community? What practical steps can you take to foster inclusivity and hospitality?

5. **Encouragement**: How can you encourage and uplift others in your community? What can you

do to create a more supportive and positive atmosphere?

Active Citizenship

1. **Being "Salt and Light"**: How can you positively influence your community and society? What actions can you take to let your "light" shine before others?

2. **Advocating for Justice**: What social justice issues are you passionate about? How can you advocate for policies and practices that promote justice and equity?

3. **Civic Duties**: How can you fulfill your civic responsibilities more effectively? What steps can you take to engage in the political process and contribute to community life?

4. **Loving Your Neighbor**: How can you actively seek the welfare of your community and address the needs of those around you? What practical acts of service can you undertake to demonstrate love for your neighbors?

5. **Peacemaking**: What steps can you take to promote peace and reconciliation within your community? How can you help resolve conflicts and build bridges between different groups?

Reflecting on these questions can help individuals understand and apply the principles of building a strong community and active citizenship, fostering a sense of unity, purpose, and mutual care.

Personal Growth and Self-Improvement

Continuous Improvement and Resilience and Perseverance

Continuous Improvement

Continuous improvement is a lifelong commitment to personal growth and the development of one's abilities, character, and spiritual life. Jesus' teachings emphasize the importance of striving for excellence, learning from mistakes, and growing in faith and character. By examining His sayings and actions, we can gain valuable insights into the principles of continuous improvement and apply them to our own lives.

1. The Call to Perfection

Jesus sets a high standard for personal growth and moral excellence.

- **Matthew 5:48**: "Be perfect, therefore, as your heavenly Father is perfect."

  - **Striving for Excellence**: This verse calls for a continuous effort towards moral and spiritual perfection, encouraging believers to constantly improve and refine their character.

- ○ **Holistic Growth**: The call to perfection encompasses all areas of life, including our thoughts, actions, relationships, and spiritual practices.

2. Parable of the Talents

Jesus emphasizes the importance of using and developing our talents and abilities.

- **Matthew 25:14-30**: In the Parable of the Talents, Jesus tells of a master who entrusts his servants with varying amounts of money (talents) and rewards those who use and grow their resources effectively.

  - ○ **Active Stewardship**: This parable teaches the importance of actively developing and utilizing our gifts and resources to achieve growth and success.

  - ○ **Accountability and Growth**: It also underscores the principle of accountability, where we are responsible for making the most of what we have been given.

3. Learning from Mistakes

Jesus teaches that growth often comes from learning from our mistakes and failures.

- **John 8:11**: When Jesus forgives the woman

caught in adultery, He tells her, "Go now and leave your life of sin."

- ○ **Repentance and Change**: This interaction emphasizes the importance of recognizing our mistakes, repenting, and making positive changes in our lives.

- ○ **Forgiveness and New Beginnings**: Jesus' forgiveness offers the opportunity for a fresh start, encouraging continuous improvement despite past failures.

4. The Importance of Humility

Humility is crucial for personal growth and continuous improvement.

- **Matthew 23:12**: "For those who exalt themselves will be humbled, and those who humble themselves will be exalted."

- ○ **Openness to Learning**: Humility involves recognizing our limitations and being open to learning and growth.

- ○ **Teachability**: A humble attitude makes us more receptive to feedback and guidance, which are essential for continuous improvement.

5. Seeking Wisdom

Jesus valued wisdom and understanding, encouraging His followers to seek and grow in knowledge.

- **Matthew 7:7**: "Ask and it will be given to you; seek and you will find; knock and the door will be opened to you."

  - **Pursuit of Knowledge**: This verse encourages the active pursuit of knowledge and wisdom, emphasizing that continuous improvement involves seeking out new understanding and insights.

  - **Divine Guidance**: It also highlights the importance of seeking divine guidance and wisdom through prayer and reflection.

6. Discipline and Self-Control

Jesus teaches the importance of discipline and self-control in personal growth.

- **Luke 9:23**: "Whoever wants to be my disciple must deny themselves and take up their cross daily and follow me."

  - **Daily Commitment**: Continuous improvement requires daily discipline and the willingness to make sacrifices for growth and development.

- ○ **Self-Control**: Practicing self-control helps us overcome obstacles and stay focused on our goals.

7. Developing Character

Jesus emphasizes the importance of developing character traits such as love, patience, and kindness.

- **Galatians 5:22-23**: Paul, reflecting Jesus' teachings, lists the fruits of the Spirit: "But the fruit of the Spirit is love, joy, peace, forbearance, kindness, goodness, faithfulness, gentleness and self-control."

  - ○ **Character Growth**: Continuous improvement involves cultivating these virtues, which reflect Christ-like character and enhance our relationships and interactions.

  - ○ **Spiritual Growth**: Developing these traits also contributes to our spiritual growth and alignment with God's will.

8. Perseverance and Endurance

Jesus teaches that perseverance is essential for achieving continuous improvement.

- **James 1:2-4**: "Consider it pure joy, my brothers and sisters, whenever you face trials of many kinds, because you know that the testing of

your faith produces perseverance. Let perseverance finish its work so that you may be mature
and complete, not lacking anything."

- **Embracing Challenges**: Continuous improvement often involves facing and overcoming challenges, which build resilience and
  strength.

- **Endurance**: Perseverance helps us to keep
  pushing forward, even when progress is slow
  or difficult.

9. Faith and Spiritual Growth

Faith is a fundamental aspect of continuous improvement
in Jesus' teachings.

- **Matthew 17:20**: "He replied, 'Because you have
  so little faith. Truly I tell you, if you have faith
  as small as a mustard seed, you can say to this
  mountain, 'Move from here to there,' and it will
  move. Nothing will be impossible for you.'"

  - **Growing in Faith**: Continuous improve-
    ment involves growing in faith and trust in
    God's power and guidance.

  - **Spiritual Confidence**: A strong faith pro-
    vides the confidence and assurance needed to
    pursue growth and overcome obstacles.

10. Community and Accountability

Jesus highlights the importance of community and accountability in personal growth.

- **Hebrews 10:24-25**: "And let us consider how we may spur one another on toward love and good deeds, not giving up meeting together, as some are in the habit of doing, but encouraging one another—and all the more as you see the Day approaching."

  - **Support Systems**: Being part of a supportive community encourages continuous improvement through mutual encouragement and accountability.

  - **Shared Growth**: Engaging with others in the pursuit of growth fosters a collaborative environment where everyone can develop and improve.

Resilience and Perseverance

Resilience and perseverance are vital aspects of personal growth and self-improvement. They involve the ability to withstand adversity, recover from setbacks, and persist in the face of challenges. Jesus' teachings and life provide profound insights into the principles of resilience and perseverance, encouraging believers to remain steadfast in their faith and actions.

1. Jesus' Example of Perseverance

Jesus' life exemplified perseverance, particularly in the face of suffering and opposition.

- **Hebrews 12:2**: "Fixing our eyes on Jesus, the pioneer and perfecter of faith. For the joy set before him, he endured the cross, scorning its shame, and sat down at the right hand of the throne of God."

    - **Endurance of the Cross**: Jesus endured the immense suffering of the crucifixion for the sake of humanity's redemption. His perseverance through this ultimate trial serves as a powerful example.

    - **Joy and Purpose**: Despite the suffering, Jesus focused on the joy set before Him—the fulfillment of God's plan and the salvation of mankind.

2. Teachings on Persistence in Prayer

Jesus encouraged persistence, especially in prayer, as a key aspect of resilience.

- **Luke 18:1-8**: The Parable of the Persistent Widow illustrates the importance of not giving up in prayer. Jesus tells of a widow who repeatedly approaches an unjust judge until he grants her request.

- **Unwavering Faith**: The widow's persistence despite initial refusal demonstrates unwavering faith and determination.

- **God's Justice**: Jesus assures that, unlike the unjust judge, God will respond to persistent prayer with justice and compassion.

3. Facing Persecution and Challenges

Jesus prepared His followers for the reality of facing persecution and challenges, urging them to persevere.

- **Matthew 5:10-12**: "Blessed are those who are persecuted because of righteousness, for theirs is the kingdom of heaven. Blessed are you when people insult you, persecute you and falsely say all kinds of evil against you because of me. Rejoice and be glad, because great is your reward in heaven..."

  - **Blessing in Persecution**: Jesus acknowledges the difficulties of persecution but promises blessings and rewards for those who endure.

  - **Rejoicing in Trials**: He encourages rejoicing in the face of adversity, viewing it as an opportunity to demonstrate faithfulness.

4. Encouragement to Stand Firm

Jesus and the apostles repeatedly encourage believers to stand firm and not lose heart.

- **John 16:33**: "I have told you these things, so that

in me you may have peace. In this world you will have trouble. But take heart! I have overcome the world."

- ○ **Overcoming the World**: Jesus assures His followers that despite the inevitable troubles in the world, they can find peace in Him and be encouraged by His victory.

- ○ **Finding Peace**: This assurance provides a foundation for resilience, knowing that Jesus has ultimately overcome all difficulties.

5. Building on Solid Foundations

Jesus teaches the importance of building our lives on solid foundations to withstand life's storms.

- • **Matthew 7:24-27**: The Parable of the Wise and Foolish Builders emphasizes the need to build on the solid rock of Jesus' teachings. The house built on the rock withstands the storms, while the one built on sand collapses.

  - ○ **Solid Foundations**: Resilience involves grounding our lives in strong, unshakeable foundations, such as faith and the teachings of Jesus.

  - ○ **Preparation for Adversity**: By adhering to Jesus' words, we prepare ourselves to face and withstand life's challenges.

6. The Role of Faith in Perseverance

Faith plays a crucial role in fostering perseverance and resilience.

- **James 1:2-4**: "Consider it pure joy, my brothers and sisters, whenever you face trials of many kinds, because you know that the testing of your faith produces perseverance. Let perseverance finish its work so that you may be mature and complete, not lacking anything."

  - **Joy in Trials**: Viewing trials as opportunities for growth and maturity helps in developing resilience.

  - **Maturity through Perseverance**: Faith tested through trials leads to a more mature and complete character.

7. Support from the Community

The community of believers plays a vital role in supporting and encouraging resilience and perseverance.

- **Hebrews 10:24-25**: "And let us consider how we may spur one another on toward love and good deeds, not giving up meeting together, as some are in the habit of doing, but encouraging one another—and all the more as you see the Day approaching."

- ○ **Mutual Encouragement**: Encouragement from others helps individuals to persevere through difficult times.

- ○ **Strength in Unity**: Regular fellowship and mutual support strengthen resilience within the community.

8. Hope and Future Glory

Jesus and the apostles often pointed to future hope and glory as motivation for perseverance.

- • **Romans 8:18**: "I consider that our present sufferings are not worth comparing with the glory that will be revealed in us."

  - ○ **Eternal Perspective**: Keeping an eternal perspective and focusing on future glory provides motivation to endure present hardships.

  - ○ **Hope in God's Promises**: The promise of future glory and eternal life strengthens resilience by providing hope and assurance.

Conclusion

Continuous Improvement

Continuous improvement is a lifelong commitment to personal growth in all areas of life, including character, abilities, and spiritual life. Jesus' teachings emphasize striving for excellence, learning from mistakes, and growing in faith and character. By setting high standards, using and developing our talents, and embracing humility, we can pursue continuous improvement, becoming more aligned with God's will and better equipped to serve others.

Resilience and Perseverance

Resilience and perseverance are essential for personal growth and self-improvement. Jesus' life and teachings provide a powerful framework for understanding and cultivating these qualities. By following His example of enduring suffering, persisting in prayer, facing challenges with faith, and building our lives on solid foundations, we can develop the strength and determination to persevere through life's trials. Supported by a community of believers and motivated by the hope of future glory, we can remain steadfast and grow in resilience.

Reflective Questions

Continuous Improvement

1. **Striving for Excellence**: In what areas of your life can you strive for greater excellence? How can you set higher standards for yourself in these areas?

2. **Using Talents**: What talents and abilities has God entrusted to you? How can you develop and

use these talents more effectively for His glory and the benefit of others?

3. **Learning from Mistakes**: Reflect on a recent mistake or failure. What lessons can you learn from this experience, and how can you apply them to improve in the future?

4. **Seeking Wisdom**: How can you actively seek wisdom and understanding in your daily life? What steps can you take to pursue knowledge and grow in your faith?

Resilience and Perseverance

1. **Facing Challenges**: What challenges are you currently facing? How can you apply Jesus' teachings on perseverance to navigate these difficulties?

2. **Persistent Prayer**: How persistent are you in your prayer life? What can you do to strengthen your commitment to prayer, especially in times of trial?

3. **Support System**: Who in your community supports you in your journey of faith? How can you strengthen these relationships and also support others in their struggles?

4. **Eternal Perspective**: How does focusing on the hope of future glory help you endure present

hardships? What can you do to keep this eternal perspective in mind during challenging times?

Reflecting on these questions can help individuals apply the principles of continuous improvement, and resilience and perseverance, fostering personal growth and spiritual maturity.

Human Rights and Dignity

Respect for Human Dignity and Justice and Fair Treatment

Respect for Human Dignity

Respect for human dignity is a fundamental principle in Jesus' teachings and the Christian faith. It involves recognizing and honoring every individual's inherent worth and value, regardless of their background, status, or circumstances. Jesus' life and teachings provide a profound framework for understanding and practicing respect for human dignity.

1. Created in God's Image

The Bible teaches that every human being is created in God's image, which is the foundation of human dignity.

- **Genesis 1:27**: "So God created mankind in his own image, in the image of God he created them; male and female he created them."

  - **Inherent Worth**: Being made in God's image confers intrinsic worth and dignity to every person.

  ○ **Universal Respect**: This teaching under-
    scores the need to respect and value everyone,
    recognizing their unique and divine origins.

2. Jesus' Compassion for the Marginalized

Jesus consistently demonstrated compassion and respect
for those marginalized by society.

  • **Matthew 9:36**: "When he saw the crowds, he had
    compassion on them, because they were harassed
    and helpless, like sheep without a shepherd."

  ○ **Compassionate Leadership**: Jesus' compas-
    sion for the crowds illustrates His deep con-
    cern for their well-being and dignity.

  ○ **Inclusivity**: Jesus' actions show that respect
    for human dignity extends to everyone, espe-
    cially the marginalized and oppressed.

3. Parable of the Good Samaritan

The Parable of the Good Samaritan emphasizes the importance of recognizing and respecting the dignity of others, regardless of social or ethnic barriers.

  • **Luke 10:25-37**: In this parable, a Samaritan
    helps a beaten man left on the road while others
    pass by without assisting.

  ○ **Breaking Barriers**: The Samaritan's actions
    highlight the importance of breaking down

social and ethnic barriers to help those in need.

- ○ **Act of Mercy**: This parable teaches that true respect for human dignity involves acts of mercy and kindness to anyone in need.

4. Jesus' Interaction with the Woman at the Well

Jesus' respectful interaction with the Samaritan woman at the well demonstrates His recognition of her dignity despite societal norms.

- **John 4:7-26**: Jesus speaks with a Samaritan woman, breaking cultural and gender barriers of His time.

  - ○ **Valuing Individuals**: By engaging with her, Jesus acknowledges her worth and dignity, challenging the societal norms that marginalized her.

  - ○ **Offering Living Water**: Jesus offers her "living water," symbolizing spiritual nourishment and respect for her spiritual needs.

5. Healing and Restoration

Jesus' healing miracles often restored individuals to their communities, affirming their dignity and value.

- **Mark 1:40-42**: Jesus heals a man with leprosy, saying, "I am willing... Be clean!" The leprosy left him immediately, and he was cleansed.

- ○ **Restoration to Community**: By healing the leper, Jesus restores his dignity and his place in society, demonstrating that physical and social restoration are intertwined.

- ○ **Holistic Healing**: Jesus' healings address both physical ailments and the social isolation caused by illness, affirming the comprehensive nature of human dignity.

6. Condemnation of Hypocrisy and Injustice

Jesus condemned hypocrisy and injustice, advocating for fair and just treatment of all individuals.

- **Matthew 23:23**: "Woe to you, teachers of the law and Pharisees, you hypocrites! You give a tenth of your spices—mint, dill, and cumin. But you have neglected the more important matters of the law—justice, mercy and faithfulness."

  - ○ **Justice and Mercy**: Jesus criticizes religious leaders for neglecting justice and mercy, highlighting the importance of fair and compassionate treatment.

  - ○ **Ethical Conduct**: His condemnation of hypocrisy underscores the need for integrity and respect in all interactions.

7. Teaching on Servanthood

Jesus taught that true greatness comes from serving others and recognizing their dignity and worth.

- **Mark 10:42-45**: "Instead, whoever wants to become great among you must be your servant, and whoever wants to be first must be slave of all. For even the Son of Man did not come to be served, but to serve, and to give his life as a ransom for many."

  - **Servant Leadership**: Jesus' model of servanthood teaches that leaders should honor the dignity of others by serving them selflessly.

  - **Equality and Respect**: This teaching promotes a community where all individuals are treated with respect and dignity, regardless of their position.

8. Respecting the Vulnerable

Jesus showed special concern for the vulnerable, including children, the poor, and the outcasts.

- **Matthew 19:14**: "Let the little children come to me, and do not hinder them, for the kingdom of heaven belongs to such as these."

  - **Value of the Vulnerable**: Jesus' welcoming of children underscores the importance of respecting and valuing the most vulnerable members of society.

○ **Inclusive Kingdom**: His teachings highlight that everyone, regardless of their status or vulnerability, has inherent dignity and value in God's kingdom.

9. Teaching on Love and Neighborliness

Jesus' command to love our neighbors as ourselves is a cornerstone of respecting human dignity.

- **Matthew 22:39**: "And the second is like it: 'Love your neighbor as yourself.'"

   ○ **Universal Love**: This commandment calls for unconditional love and respect for others, recognizing their intrinsic worth.

   ○ **Empathy and Respect**: Loving others as ourselves involves empathy, respect, and a commitment to their well-being.

10. Judgment and Dignity

Jesus taught that our treatment of others will be a basis for judgment, emphasizing the importance of respecting human dignity.

- **Matthew 25:40**: "The King will reply, 'Truly I tell you, whatever you did for one of the least of these brothers and sisters of mine, you did for me.'"

   ○ **Eternal Perspective**: Jesus links respect for

human dignity with eternal consequences, highlighting its importance in God's eyes.

- ○ **Service to Others**: Our actions toward others, especially the least and the vulnerable, are seen as direct service to Christ Himself.

Justice and Fair Treatment

Justice and fair treatment are central themes in Jesus' teachings and the broader biblical narrative. Jesus consistently advocated for justice, denounced hypocrisy, and emphasized the importance of treating others with fairness and equity. His life and teachings provide profound insights into how we can pursue justice and fair treatment in our personal lives and society.

1. Jesus' Mission of Justice

Jesus' mission was deeply rooted in the principles of justice and liberation for the oppressed.

- • **Luke 4:18-19**: "The Spirit of the Lord is on me, because he has anointed me to proclaim good news to the poor. He has sent me to proclaim freedom for the prisoners and recovery of sight for the blind, to set the oppressed free, to proclaim the year of the Lord's favor."

  - ○ **Liberation and Healing**: Jesus' mission includes proclaiming freedom and setting the oppressed free, highlighting His commitment to justice and liberation.

- ○ **Good News for the Poor**: His message is particularly focused on the marginalized, ensuring they receive fair treatment and justice.

2. Condemnation of Hypocrisy and Injustice

Jesus often condemned the religious leaders for their hypocrisy and failure to uphold true justice.

- **Matthew 23:23-24**: "Woe to you, teachers of the law and Pharisees, you hypocrites! You give a tenth of your spices—mint, dill and cumin. But you have neglected the more important matters of the law—justice, mercy and faithfulness. You should have practiced the latter, without neglecting the former."

  - ○ **True Justice**: Jesus criticizes the Pharisees for neglecting the core principles of justice, mercy, and faithfulness, emphasizing their importance over ritualistic practices.

  - ○ **Integrity and Fairness**: His denunciation highlights the need for integrity and fairness in all dealings.

3. The Golden Rule

The Golden Rule is a fundamental principle of fair treatment and justice in Jesus' teachings.

- **Matthew 7:12**: "So in everything, do to others what you would have them do to you, for this sums up the Law and the Prophets."

  - **Reciprocal Fairness**: Treating others as we wish to be treated fosters mutual respect and justice.

  - **Ethical Guideline**: This principle serves as an ethical guideline for ensuring fair treatment in all interactions.

4. Parable of the Workers in the Vineyard

This parable illustrates God's justice and fairness, challenging human notions of entitlement and fairness.

- **Matthew 20:1-16**: In the Parable of the Workers in the Vineyard, a landowner pays all his workers the same wage, regardless of how long they worked.

  - **Divine Justice**: This parable underscores that God's justice may differ from human expectations but remains inherently fair.

  - **Equality and Generosity**: It teaches about the equality of all in God's eyes and the importance of generosity.

5. Judging Others

Jesus teaches about the importance of fairness and humility when judging others.

- **Matthew 7:1-2**: "Do not judge, or you too will be judged. For in the same way you judge others, you will be judged, and with the measure you use, it will be measured to you."

    ○ **Fair Judgment**: This teaching emphasizes the need for fairness and humility, warning against hypocrisy and harsh judgment.

    ○ **Self-Reflection**: It encourages self-reflection and fair treatment of others, recognizing our own flaws.

6. Parable of the Good Samaritan

This parable is a powerful example of justice, compassion, and fair treatment.

- **Luke 10:25-37**: The Parable of the Good Samaritan tells of a Samaritan who helps a man beaten and left for dead while others pass by without helping.

    ○ **Compassionate Justice**: The Samaritan's actions exemplify true justice and compassion, going beyond societal prejudices to help someone in need.

- ○ **Universal Neighborliness**: This parable teaches that justice and fair treatment should extend to all, regardless of ethnic or social boundaries.

7. Jesus and the Woman Caught in Adultery

Jesus' response to the woman caught in adultery demonstrates justice tempered with mercy.

- **John 8:1-11**: When a woman caught in adultery is brought to Jesus, He challenges those without sin to cast the first stone, ultimately telling her to "go and sin no more."

  - ○ **Merciful Justice**: Jesus prevents an unjust execution and offers the woman a chance for redemption, blending justice with mercy.

  - ○ **Condemnation of Hypocrisy**: His response also highlights the hypocrisy of those who condemned her while being guilty of their own sins.

8. Jesus' Teachings on Wealth and Fairness

Jesus often spoke about wealth, fairness, and the responsibility of the rich to act justly.

- **Luke 16:19-31**: The Parable of the Rich Man and Lazarus contrasts the lives of a wealthy man and a poor beggar, Lazarus. The rich man's neglect of Lazarus leads to his eternal suffering.

- **Social Responsibility**: This parable emphasizes the duty of the wealthy to act justly and compassionately toward the poor.

- **Eternal Consequences**: It underscores the eternal consequences of failing to treat others with fairness and justice.

9. Teaching on Servant Leadership

Jesus teaches that true leadership involves serving others, emphasizing fairness and humility.

- **Mark 10:42-45**: "Instead, whoever wants to become great among you must be your servant, and whoever wants to be first must be slave of all."

  - **Servant Leadership**: Jesus redefines leadership as serving others, highlighting that fair and just treatment is essential for true leadership.

  - **Humility in Leadership**: This teaching promotes humility and fairness in positions of authority.

Conclusion

Respect for Human Dignity

Respect for human dignity is a fundamental principle in Jesus' teachings. By recognizing that all people are created in God's image and treating them with compassion, respect, and justice, we honor their inherent worth and value. Jesus' life and teachings provide a profound framework for understanding and respecting human dignity, guiding us to serve others selflessly, break down social barriers, and advocate for justice and mercy.

Justice and Fair Treatment

Justice and fair treatment are central to Jesus' teachings, emphasizing the importance of integrity, compassion, and equality in all interactions. Through His mission of justice, condemnation of hypocrisy, and parables, Jesus demonstrates the need for fair treatment of all individuals. His teachings encourage us to practice reciprocal fairness, judge others with humility, and uphold the principles of justice in our daily lives. By following Jesus' example, we can promote a just and equitable society that honors the dignity of every person.

Reflective Questions

Respect for Human Dignity

1. **Inherent Worth**: How can you better recognize and honor the inherent worth and dignity of those around you?

2. **Compassion for the Marginalized**: In what ways can you show compassion and respect for marginalized individuals in your community?

3. **Breaking Barriers**: How can you work to break down social and ethnic barriers that prevent the full recognition of human dignity?

4. **Acts of Mercy**: What practical acts of mercy and kindness can you perform to demonstrate respect for human dignity?

5. **Servant Leadership**: How can you practice servant leadership in your daily life, honoring the dignity and worth of those you lead or serve?

Justice and Fair Treatment

1. **Advocating for Justice**: What actions can you take to advocate for justice and fair treatment in your community?

2. **Fair Judgment**: How can you ensure that your judgments of others are fair and free of hypocrisy?

3. **Compassionate Action**: In what ways can you demonstrate compassion and justice in your interactions with others?

4. **Social Responsibility**: How can you use your resources and influence to promote fairness and justice for the less privileged?

5. **Servant Leadership**: What steps can you take to embody servant leadership and ensure fair treatment of those you lead or influence?

Reflecting on these questions can help individuals apply Jesus' teachings on respect for human dignity and justice ,and fair treatment, fostering a more just, compassionate, and inclusive society.

Spiritual and Moral Foundations

Spiritual Fulfillment and Ethical Living

Spiritual Fulfillment

Spiritual fulfillment is the sense of deep satisfaction, peace, and purpose that comes from a close relationship with God and living according to His will. Jesus' teachings provide profound insights into achieving spiritual fulfillment, emphasizing the importance of seeking God's Kingdom, developing a relationship with Him, and living a life of faith and obedience.

1. Seeking First the Kingdom of God

Jesus emphasizes the importance of prioritizing spiritual pursuits over material concerns.

- **Matthew 6:33**: "But seek first his kingdom and his righteousness, and all these things will be given to you as well."

    - **Primary Focus**: Jesus teaches that focusing on God's Kingdom and His righteousness should be our primary concern, with the assurance that our material needs will be met.

- **Divine Priorities**: Spiritual fulfillment comes from aligning our priorities with God's, putting spiritual growth and obedience at the forefront of our lives.

2. Developing a Relationship with God

A close, personal relationship with God is central to spiritual fulfillment.

- **John 15:4**: "Remain in me, as I also remain in you. No branch can bear fruit by itself; it must remain in the vine. Neither can you bear fruit unless you remain in me."

  - **Abiding in Christ**: Jesus illustrates the necessity of maintaining a close, abiding relationship with Him by using the metaphor of the vine and branches.

  - **Fruitfulness**: Spiritual fulfillment and fruitful living are outcomes of this deep connection with Christ as we draw spiritual nourishment from Him.

3. The Bread of Life

Jesus describes Himself as the source of spiritual sustenance and fulfillment.

- **John 6:35**: "Then Jesus declared, 'I am the bread of life. Whoever comes to me will never go hun-

gry, and whoever believes in me will never be thi
rsty.'"

○ **Spiritual Nourishment**: Jesus offers Himself as the ultimate source of spiritual sustenance, satisfying our deepest spiritual needs
and longings.

○ **Fulfillment in Christ**: True fulfillment is
found in a relationship with Jesus, who provides for our spiritual hunger and thirst.

4. Living Water

Jesus promises the gift of the Holy Spirit, symbolized as
living water, which brings spiritual renewal and fulfillment.

• **John 4:13-14**: "Jesus answered, 'Everyone who
drinks this water will be thirsty again, but whoever drinks the water I give them will never thirst.
Indeed, the water I give them will become in them
a spring of water welling up to eternal life.'"

○ **Holy Spirit**: The living water represents the
Holy Spirit, who dwells within believers, providing ongoing spiritual renewal and fulfillment.

○ **Eternal Satisfaction**: This living water leads
to eternal life and continual spiritual satisfaction, unlike temporary earthly pleasures.

5. The Beatitudes

The Beatitudes outline the attitudes and behaviors that lead to spiritual fulfillment and blessings.

- **Matthew 5:3-12**: Jesus begins the Sermon on the Mount with the Beatitudes, describing the blessed state of those who exhibit qualities like humility, mercy, purity, and peacemaking.

  - **Blessedness**: Each Beatitude highlights a different aspect of spiritual fulfillment, demonstrating that true happiness and fulfillment come from living in accordance with God's values.

  - **Kingdom Values**: The Beatitudes provide a blueprint for a life that is spiritually fulfilled and aligned with the values of God's Kingdom.

6. Rest for the Weary

Jesus invites those who are burdened to find rest and fulfillment in Him.

- **Matthew 11:28-30**: "Come to me, all you who are weary and burdened, and I will give you rest. Take my yoke upon you and learn from me, for I am gentle and humble in heart, and you will find rest for your souls. For my yoke is easy and my burden is light."

○ **Invitation to Rest**: Jesus offers rest and relief to those who are spiritually weary, promising a light burden and an easy yoke.

○ **Gentleness and Humility**: By learning from Jesus and adopting His gentle and humble ways, we find spiritual peace and fulfillment.

7. Purpose and Mission

Jesus provides a sense of purpose and mission, which is essential for spiritual fulfillment.

• **Matthew 28:19-20**: "Therefore go and make disciples of all nations, baptizing them in the name of the Father and of the Son and of the Holy Spirit, and teaching them to obey everything I have commanded you. And surely I am with you always, to the very end of the age."

○ **Great Commission**: Jesus' Great Commission gives believers a clear purpose and mission, contributing to a sense of spiritual fulfillment through active discipleship and teaching.

○ **Ongoing Presence**: The assurance of Jesus' continual presence provides comfort and fulfillment as we carry out His mission.

8. Prayer and Communion with God

Jesus teaches the importance of prayer as a means of deepening our relationship with God and finding spiritual fulfillment.

- **Matthew 6:6**: "But when you pray, go into your room, close the door and pray to your Father, who is unseen. Then your Father, who sees what is done in secret, will reward you."

  - **Private Prayer**: Jesus emphasizes the value of private, sincere prayer, which fosters a deeper, more intimate relationship with God.

  - **Divine Reward**: The reward of prayer is spiritual fulfillment and a closer connection with our Heavenly Father.

9. Spiritual Transformation

Jesus calls for a transformation of the heart and mind, which leads to true spiritual fulfillment.

- **Romans 12:2**: "Do not conform to the pattern of this world, but be transformed by the renewing of your mind. Then you will be able to test and approve what God's will is—his good, pleasing and perfect will."

  - **Renewal of Mind**: Spiritual fulfillment comes from transforming and renewing our thinking, aligning our minds with God's will.

  - **Discerning God's Will**: This transformation enables us to discern and live out God's perfect will, leading to a fulfilling spiritual life.

10. Living in the Spirit

Paul, reflecting Jesus' teachings, speaks about living according to the Spirit as the path to spiritual fulfillment.

- **Galatians 5:22-23**: "But the fruit of the Spirit is love, joy, peace, forbearance, kindness, goodness, faithfulness, gentleness and self-control."

  - **Fruit of the Spirit**: Living in the Spirit produces qualities that contribute to a fulfilled and harmonious spiritual life.

  - **Spirit-Led Life**: A life led by the Holy Spirit is marked by these fruits, reflecting the character of Christ and leading to true spiritual fulfillment.

11. Peace and Contentment

Jesus teaches that true peace and contentment are found in Him, not in worldly possessions or achievements.

- **John 14:27**: "Peace I leave with you; my peace I give you. I do not give to you as the world gives. Do not let your hearts be troubled and do not be afraid."

  - **Divine Peace**: Jesus offers a peace that surpasses worldly understanding, providing deep contentment and tranquility.

○ **Freedom from Fear**: This peace helps to overcome fear and anxiety, contributing to a fulfilled spiritual life.

Ethical Living

Ethical living involves adhering to moral principles and values in our daily actions and decisions. Jesus' teachings provide a profound framework for ethical living, emphasizing love, integrity, compassion, justice, and humility. By following His example and teachings, we can live lives that reflect God's will and promote the well-being of others.

1. The Greatest Commandments

Jesus summarizes the entire Law with two foundational ethical principles.

- **Matthew 22:37-40**: "Jesus replied: 'Love the Lord your God with all your heart and with all your soul and with all your mind.' This is the first and greatest commandment. And the second is like it: 'Love your neighbor as yourself.' All the Law and the Prophets hang on these two commandments."

    ○ **Love for God and Others**: Ethical living begins with love for God and extends to love for others. This love should guide all our actions and decisions.

    ○ **Foundational Principles**: These two commandments serve as the foundation for all ethical behavior, encapsulating the essence of Jesus' teachings.

2. The Golden Rule

Jesus provides a simple yet profound guideline for ethical conduct.

- **Matthew 7:12**: "So in everything, do to others what you would have them do to you, for this sums up the Law and the Prophets."

  - **Reciprocity and Empathy**: Treating others as we would like to be treated fosters empathy, respect, and fairness in our interactions.

  - **Practical Ethics**: The Golden Rule offers a practical approach to ethical living that is applicable in all situations.

3. Integrity and Honesty

Jesus emphasizes the importance of honesty and integrity in all aspects of life.

- **Matthew 5:37**: "All you need to say is simply 'Yes' or 'No'; anything beyond this comes from the evil one."

  - **Truthfulness**: Being truthful and straightforward in our communication builds trust and reflects ethical integrity.

- ○ **Consistency in Actions**: Integrity involves aligning our actions with our words and maintaining consistency in our ethical standards.

4. Compassion and Mercy

Jesus teaches the importance of showing compassion and mercy to others.

- **Matthew 5:7**: "Blessed are the merciful, for they will be shown mercy."

  - ○ **Acts of Kindness**: Ethical living includes performing acts of kindness and showing mercy to those in need.

  - ○ **Reflecting God's Character**: By being merciful, we reflect God's character and His compassionate nature.

5. Justice and Fair Treatment

Jesus advocates for justice and fair treatment of all individuals.

- **Matthew 23:23**: "Woe to you, teachers of the law and Pharisees, you hypocrites! You give a tenth of your spices—mint, dill and cumin. But you have neglected the more important matters of the law—justice, mercy and faithfulness."

  - ○ **Pursuing Justice**: Ethical living involves actively pursuing justice and ensuring fair treatment for everyone.

- ○ **Addressing Injustice**: This includes standing against injustice and advocating for those who are marginalized or oppressed.

6. Humility and Service

Jesus exemplifies humility and calls His followers to serve others selflessly.

- **Mark 10:43-45**: "Not so with you. Instead, whoever wants to become great among you must be your servant, and whoever wants to be first must be slave of all. For even the Son of Man did not come to be served, but to serve, and to give his life as a ransom for many."

  - ○ **Servant Leadership**: Ethical living involves serving others with humility and placing their needs above our own.

  - ○ **Following Jesus' Example**: Jesus' life of service and sacrifice provides a model for how we should live ethically.

7. Forgiveness and Reconciliation

Jesus emphasizes the importance of forgiveness and reconciliation in maintaining ethical relationships.

- **Matthew 6:14-15**: "For if you forgive other people when they sin against you, your heavenly Father will also forgive you. But if you do not forgive others their sins, your Father will not forgive your sins."

- **Restoring Relationships**: Ethical living involves forgiving others and seeking reconciliation to restore broken relationships.

- **Removing Resentment**: Forgiveness helps remove resentment and fosters peace and harmony.

8. Avoiding Hypocrisy

Jesus condemns hypocrisy and calls for genuine, sincere living.

- **Matthew 23:27-28**: "Woe to you, teachers of the law and Pharisees, you hypocrites! You are like whitewashed tombs, which look beautiful on the outside but on the inside are full of the bones of the dead and everything unclean. In the same way, on the outside you appear to people as righteous but on the inside you are full of hypocrisy and wickedness."

  - **Authenticity**: Ethical living requires authenticity and sincerity, avoiding the pretense of righteousness.

  - **Inner Purity**: It involves cultivating inner purity and aligning our outward actions with our inner values.

9. Peacemaking

Jesus calls His followers to be peacemakers, promoting peace and harmony in their communities.

- **Matthew 5:9**: "Blessed are the peacemakers, for they will be called children of God."

  ○ **Promoting Peace**: Ethical living includes actively promoting peace and resolving conflicts.

  ○ **Building Harmony**: Peacemaking efforts contribute to building harmonious relationships and communities.

10. Stewardship of Resources

Jesus teaches responsible stewardship of the resources and talents entrusted to us.

- **Matthew 25:14-30**: The Parable of the Talents highlights the importance of using our resources wisely and responsibly.

  ○ **Accountability**: Ethical living involves being accountable for how we manage our resources and opportunities.

  ○ **Maximizing Potential**: It also includes striving to maximize the potential of the gifts and talents we have been given.

Conclusion

Spiritual Fulfillment

Spiritual fulfillment is achieved through a close relationship with God, prioritizing His Kingdom, and living a life of faith and obedience. Jesus' teachings emphasize the importance of seeking God, developing a personal relationship with Him, and finding true satisfaction in His presence. By following Jesus' example, believers can experience deep spiritual fulfillment, peace, and purpose.

Ethical Living

Ethical living involves adhering to moral principles and values in our daily actions and decisions. Jesus' teachings provide a comprehensive framework for ethical living, emphasizing love, integrity, compassion, justice, and humility. By following His example and teachings, we can live lives that reflect God's will, promote the well-being of others, and contribute to a just and compassionate society.

Reflective Questions

Spiritual Fulfillment

1. **Prioritizing God's Kingdom**: How can you prioritize seeking God's Kingdom and His right-

eousness in your daily life?

2. **Abiding in Christ**: What steps can you take to deepen your relationship with Christ and remain in Him?

3. **Spiritual Nourishment**: How can you regularly nourish your spiritual life to ensure you remain fulfilled and satisfied in Christ?

4. **Purpose and Mission**: How do you understand and engage with the mission Jesus has given to His followers?

5. **Prayer Life**: How can you improve your prayer life to foster a deeper communion with God and enhance your spiritual fulfillment?

Ethical Living

1. **Love and Compassion**: How can you better demonstrate love and compassion in your interactions with others?

2. **Integrity and Honesty**: What areas of your life require greater integrity and honesty?

3. **Justice and Fair Treatment**: How can you actively pursue justice and ensure fair treatment for those around you?

4. **Servant Leadership**: How can you embody the

principles of servant leadership in your community or workplace?

5. **Forgiveness and Reconciliation**: Are there any relationships in your life that need healing through forgiveness and reconciliation?

Reflecting on these questions can help individuals apply Jesus' teachings on spiritual fulfillment and ethical living, fostering a deeper relationship with God and a more just and compassionate life.

Final Reflection

*Applying Jesus' Teachings in a Modern,
Technologically Advanced, Fast-Paced, Global Society*

Embracing Technology and Staying Grounded

In today's digital age, integrating Jesus' teachings with technological advancements can enhance our lives while keeping us grounded in spiritual and moral values.

- **Mindful Use of Technology**: Use technology to spread positive messages, foster community, and support social causes. Avoid getting lost in digital distractions and prioritize meaningful, real-life interactions.

- **Digital Compassion**: Show kindness and respect in online interactions. Treat others with the same empathy and consideration as you would in person, following the Golden Rule (Matthew 7:12).

Balancing Speed with Purpose

The fast pace of modern life often pressures us to rush through our days. Jesus' teachings remind us to find balance and purpose amidst the hustle.

- **Sabbath Rest**: Embrace the principle of rest and reflection. Taking time to pause, reflect, and recharge helps maintain mental and emotional well-being.

- **Intentional Living**: Focus on purposeful living rather than mindless busyness. Prioritize activities that align with your values and contribute to your spiritual and personal growth.

Global Citizenship

In our interconnected world, Jesus' call to love and serve transcends borders, urging us to act as global citizens.

- **Social Responsibility**: Engage in efforts that address global issues such as poverty, climate change, and human rights. Advocate for policies and practices that promote the common good.

- **Cultural Respect**: Respect and learn from diverse cultures and perspectives. Embrace the richness of global diversity, recognizing that all people are created in God's image.

The teachings of Jesus are timeless, providing guidance and wisdom that transcends the eras and the evolution of society. In our modern, technologically advanced, fast-paced, global society, His messages are not only relevant but essential for forming a good and meaningful life. Let's reflect on how these teachings can be integrated into our contemporary context to foster a life of fulfillment, integrity, and compassion.

1. Love and Compassion in a Diverse World

In a global society where diversity is more prominent than ever, Jesus' command to "love your neighbor as yourself" (Matthew 22:39) calls us to embrace inclusivity and tolerance. This means:

- **Practicing Empathy**: Technology connects us with people worldwide, but it can also create distance. Actively practicing empathy helps bridge this gap, fostering deeper connections and understanding.

- **Supporting the Marginalized**: The Parable of the Good Samaritan (Luke 10:25-37) encourages us to support those in need, advocating for social justice and humanitarian efforts. This involves engaging in community service, supporting global causes, and using technology to amplify voices that are often unheard.

2. Forgiveness and Reconciliation

In a world often divided by conflict and grudges, Jesus' emphasis on forgiveness (Matthew 6:14-15) is crucial for healing divisions and fostering peace.

- **Digital Interactions**: Online interactions can sometimes be harsh and unforgiving. Practicing forgiveness in digital spaces promotes a more positive and respectful online environment.

- **Restorative Justice**: The story of the Prodigal Son (Luke 15:11-32) highlights the power of mercy and restorative justice. Advocating for restorative practices in both personal conflicts and broader societal issues can transform lives and communities.

3. Ethical Leadership and Integrity

Jesus taught that true leadership is about serving others (Matthew 20:26-28). In today's world, ethical leadership is more important than ever.

- **Corporate and Political Leadership**: Leaders in all sectors are called to act with integrity and accountability, as outlined in the Sermon on the Mount (Matthew 5-7). Transparent and ethical behavior builds trust and fosters a healthier society.

- **Personal Integrity**: On a personal level, maintaining honesty and integrity in all actions, both online and offline, contributes to a trustworthy and ethical community.

4. Economic Justice and Fairness

Jesus' concern for the poor and disadvantaged (Matthew 25:35-40) urges modern societies to address economic inequalities.

- **Fair Distribution of Resources**: Advocating for policies that support economic justice and fair distribution of resources is crucial in a global economy.

- **Responsible Stewardship**: The Parable of the Talents (Matthew 25:14-30) emphasizes the importance of using resources wisely. This includes personal finances, business practices, and environmental stewardship, promoting sustainability and responsibility.

5. Mental and Emotional Well-being

In a world filled with stress and anxiety, Jesus' message of peace (John 14:27) offers comfort and guidance.

- **Mindfulness and Prayer**: Incorporating practices like prayer, meditation, and mindfulness can help alleviate anxiety and promote inner calm, as Jesus advised against excessive worry (Matthew 6:25-34).

- **Community Support**: Building supportive communities, both online and offline, provides a network of care and encouragement essential for mental and emotional well-being.

6. Environmental Stewardship

While Jesus did not explicitly address environmental issues, the principle of stewardship found in His teachings can be extended to caring for the environment.

- **Sustainable Living**: Embracing sustainable practices and advocating for policies that protect the environment ensure that we fulfill our role as stewards of God's creation.

- **Global Responsibility**: Recognizing our global interconnectedness, efforts to combat climate change and protect natural resources reflect our commitment to caring for creation.

7. Community and Social Responsibility

Building strong, supportive communities is vital in a time when social isolation is prevalent.

- **Active Citizenship**: Being "salt and light" in the world (Matthew 5:13-16) involves engaging in community service, volunteering, and advocating for social change, contributing positively to society.

- **Building Community**: Jesus' teachings on loving one another (John 13:34-35) and living in harmony emphasize the importance of building and nurturing strong, supportive communities.

8. Personal Growth and Self-Improvement

Jesus' call to "be perfect, therefore, as your heavenly Father is perfect" (Matthew 5:48) encourages continuous improvement and personal growth.

- **Lifelong Learning**: Embracing lifelong learning and self-improvement fosters a culture of growth and excellence.

- **Resilience and Perseverance**: Jesus' teachings on faith and perseverance (Matthew 17:20) inspire us to remain resilient in the face of challenges, pursuing our goals with determination.

9. Human Rights and Dignity

Jesus' interactions with marginalized individuals highlight the inherent dignity of every person.

- Respect for All: Advocating for human rights and equality and treating everyone with respect and dignity reflects Jesus' teachings.

- **Justice and Fair Treatment**: His denunciation of hypocrisy and injustice (Matthew 23) aligns with contemporary calls for transparency, accountability, and fair treatment in all aspects of society.

10. Spiritual and Moral Foundations

Spiritual fulfillment and ethical living are cornerstones of a meaningful life.

- **Spiritual Fulfillment**: Seeking first the Kingdom of God (Matthew 6:33) invites us to prioritize spiritual and moral values over material pursuits, offering a path to deeper fulfillment and purpose.

- **Ethical Living**: The Beatitudes (Matthew 5:3-12) provide a blueprint for ethical living, promoting values such as humility, mercy, and peacemaking.

Final Reflection

In our modern, technologically advanced, fast-paced, global society, the teachings of Jesus offer timeless guidance for forming a good life. His messages of love, compassion, justice, and integrity are as relevant today as they were two thousand years ago. By embracing these principles, we can navigate the complexities of contemporary life with grace and wisdom.

- **Embrace Diversity**: Foster inclusivity and tolerance, recognizing the value and dignity of every individual.

- **Practice Forgiveness**: Heal divisions and promote peace through forgiveness and reconciliation.

- **Lead Ethically**: Prioritize integrity and accountability in all leadership and personal conduct aspects.

- **Champion Justice**: Advocate for economic justice and fair treatment, ensuring that resources are distributed equitably.

- **Prioritize Well-being**: Cultivate mental and emotional well-being through mindfulness, community support, and faith.

- **Protect the Environment**: Engage in sustainable practices and stewardship of the Earth's resources.

- **Build Community**: Strengthen social bonds and actively contribute to the well-being of your community.

- **Pursue Growth**: Commit to continuous improvement and resilience in personal and professional life.

- **Honor Human Dignity**: Respect and advocate for the rights and dignity of all people.

- **Seek Spiritual Fulfillment**: Prioritize spiritual and moral foundations, seeking fulfillment and purpose in a relationship with God.

Conclusion

Jesus' teachings provide a timeless guide for navigating the complexities of modern life. By embracing love, compassion, justice, and integrity, we can create a world that reflects the values of God's Kingdom. In a fast-paced, technologically advanced global society, staying grounded in these principles ensures that we live purposeful, fulfilling, and ethical lives. By reflecting on these teachings and integrating them into our daily actions, we can foster a more just, compassionate, and connected world, honoring God and serving others in all we do.

About the Author

Steven Smith has been giving lessons about the Gospels since 2005. The author is an educator and lifelong student, having studied at universities in Canada and the UK. His interest in the Gospels is focused on Jesus's messages of Peace and Love. Steven's inspiration to become an educator comes from his wife, who is a university professor. They have two children, a Jack Russell Terrier, and two rescued cats.